The Psychological Impact and Traumatic Effects
of Spiritual Abuse in the Evangelical Christian Church

The Forgotten Self
Remember Who You Truly Are

Dr. Cristy S. Carr

Published by
AUTOTELICLIFE

The Forgotten Self: Remember Who You Truly Are
Copyright © Dr. Cristy S. Carr, 2025

All rights reserved. No part of this publication may be reproduced, stored in or introduced into a retrieval system, or transmitted, in any form, or by any means, (electronic, mechanical, photocopying, recording, or otherwise), without the prior written permission of the copyright owner of this content.

The scanning, uploading, and distribution of this content via the internet or via any other means without the permission of the copyright owner is illegal and punishable by law. Please purchase only authorized electronic editions, and do not participate in or encourage electronic piracy of copyrighted materials. Your support of the author's rights are appreciated.

Unless otherwise indicated, all Scripture quotations are taken from NKJV. Scripture taken from the New King James Version. Copyright © 1982 by Thomas Nelson, Inc. Used by permission. All rights reserved.

Scripture quotations marked TPT are from The Passion Translation®. Copyright © 2017, 2018, 2020 by Passion & Fire Ministries, Inc. Used by permission. All rights reserved. ThePassionTranslation.com.

Published by:

AutotelicLife.com
Redding, California

For information about special discounts for bulk purchases, please contact:
info@AutotelicLife.com

Cover + Interior Layout by BookBloks.com

Paperback ISBN: 979-8-9988191-0-0
eBook ISBN: 979-8-9988191-1-7
Library of Congress Control Number: 2025925472

Printed in the United States of America.

"*The Forgotten Self* combines intellectual rigor with heartfelt narrative, offering readers a window into both the process and the results of the research study. I am confident that Dr. Carr's work through this book will continue to make positive changes to people affected by the Evangelical Christian Church and experience spiritual abuse."

—TARA RAVA ZOLNIKOV, PhD, MS, MS, MS
Professor, Editor at Dialogues in Health Publications and Research

"*The Forgotten Self* is a book for anyone struggling to find themselves again, or for the first time, while recovering from spiritual abuse. As a survivor of high control religion, I can attest that fellow religious refugees will find Dr. Carr's work helpful and healing."

—ANONYMOUS,
Doctoral Phenomenological Study Participant

"*The Forgotten Self* is an extraordinary and thoughtfully crafted work. It reads less like a single book and more like an entire library bound together. The depth of research, historical context, clinical insight, and present day relevance is evident on every page.

What stands out most is the care with which Dr. Carr holds the reader. This book makes room for every journey. It does not dismiss faith, nor does it demand that faith be preserved. Instead, it honors choice, dignity, and the deeply personal nature of healing after spiritual harm.

The work is clearly trauma informed, clinically sound, and deeply responsible in how it names spiritual abuse and its impact. It offers language for experiences that are often confusing, isolating, and difficult to articulate, while never reducing the reader to their wounds.

This is a powerful resource for clinicians supporting clients navigating deconstruction or reconstruction. It is equally meaningful for those trying to understand a loved one who is questioning their faith, and for those who have already walked that path themselves.

Perhaps most importantly, this book reminds us that spiritual abuse is not the end of the story. What was harmed does not have to define who you are. Reconnection to self is a sacred and healing first step, and this book offers a compassionate, grounded guide for that journey. Whether faith is rediscovered, reimagined, or released, the invitation remains the same: to remember who you truly are."

—MELANIE HUGGARD,
Doctoral Phenomenological Study Participant

Dedication

With heartfelt admiration, I dedicate this book to the Souls who fell in love with Jesus—only to feel that connection slip away within the walls of an Evangelical Church.

I often share that I was first met by **LOVE**, and later sought guidance in Church believing it would deepen this sacred relationship—only to find that the Jesus who met me was not the one they taught.

To those who have entrusted me with your deepest pain, your tender hearts, and your most profound wounds, to those who have endured the existential trauma of spiritual abuse, I offer this dedication with deep compassion, gratitude, and honor. It has been my privilege to witness your resilience and to walk alongside you on this journey of healing.

You are the courageous Ones. The brave Souls who refused to forget the Truth of who Jesus is and has always been for you. You are the Ones who tenaciously chose to. . .

Remember Who You Truly Are—a Beautiful Soul, Deeply Loved

Table of Contents

Kintsugi Bowl	ix
Preface	xi
Note on Sources	xv
Introduction	xvii
Part One: *Understanding Trauma*	1
Chapter 1 | Trauma and the Impact on the Self	5
Chapter 2 | Development of the Self	25
Part One Summary	39
Part Two: *Unveiling the Wound*	43
Chapter 3 | Abuse in Christian Religion	47
Chapter 4 | Spiritual Abuse: Wounding the Immortal Soul	73
Part Two Summary	107
Part Three: *The Inner Architecture of Understanding*	111
Chapter 5 | Damaging Doctrines	115
Chapter 6 | Coming Home to Yourself	137
Part Three Summary	141
Part Four: *Reclaiming the Heart of Faith*	145
Chapter 7 | Through the Lens of Love: Challenging What We Were Taught	149
Chapter 8 | Reclaiming Your Truth	155
Part Four Summary	179
Homecoming of the Soul: *Awakening to Love, Freedom, and True Self*	183
Stepping into the Light	185
A New Beginning	189
Appendix	191
References	195
Expanded Perspectives | Recommended Reading & Listening	205
Acknowledgments	213
About the Author	215

Kintsugi Bowl

The bowl featured on the cover of *The Forgotten Self* is a visual representation of the Japanese art of Kintsugi—the practice of repairing broken pottery with gold. Rather than hiding the cracks, Kintsugi highlights them, honoring the story and transformation of the vessel. In the same way, this book invites those who have been spiritually shattered to recognize that their healing does not erase their pain but instead illuminates it with truth, beauty, and love. The gold that fills the fractures represents the soul's remembrance—that even in our most painful breaking, something sacred endures. We are not broken beyond repair. We are being re-formed in Love.

Preface

"Knowing your own darkness is the best method for dealing with the darkness of other people. One does not become enlightened by imagining figures of light, but by making the darkness conscious. The most terrifying thing is to accept oneself completely. Your visions will become clear only when you can look into your own heart.

Who looks outside, dreams; who looks inside, awakes."

—CARL JUNG

As you read these words, my deepest hope is that you feel Love pouring back to you. Please receive these words with the Love in which they are offered—from the bottom of my heart, from every fiber of my being, from the very depths of my Soul.

I do not wish any harm to any of you.

This work—this journey, this path—has been extremely painful for me to walk, because I know these words may cause discomfort. But please hear me: *this is not my desire*. This book is not intended to tell you what to believe, what to think, or how to feel. Rather, it is meant to be a guide—to invite you inward, to help you look deeply within, and *remember who you are*.

It is meant to create a safe space for you to hear your inner voice again. To heal.

For those who have come out of abusive experiences in religious communities, or from relationships with those inside them—I urge you to give yourself the grace and time to feel all that may arise. Be kind and compassionate with yourself. And when possible, please accept help from others. This path can be painful, but you are not alone. Many others are walking it with you. There is Hope. You *will* heal. You *will* hear yourself again. You *will* know who you are. Trust yourself. Be attentive to what you need.

For those of you who are still attending these communities, and may struggle to understand how harm can be caused, I thank you. Thank you for being here, for reading this, for educating yourself, and for your willingness to be curious. You are on a courageous journey—a path of Love. I honor your bravery. I honor your heart.

This research is not meant to divide us. It is not meant to accuse. My heart is to help you understand—from a place of compassion.

Please, do not use these words as fuel for judgment or further harm. I do not believe most people intend to cause pain. We are all shaped by systems—systems that have developed over centuries. The intention here is not to blame, but to *see*... and in seeing, to choose something different.

Change begins with humility. With the courage to ask hard questions:

- Have I ever participated in harmful beliefs or behaviors, knowingly or unknowingly?
- Have I judged or silenced another on their spiritual path?
- Have I clung to control when someone I loved needed freedom?
- Have I been afraid to let another grow in their own way?

These are not questions of shame. They are invitations to healing.

May these words deepen your compassion—not only for others, but most of all, for yourself. Because when we harm another, we also harm ourselves. And when we love another, we bring healing to the whole.

Let us learn to allow difference.
Let us release the need for sameness and control.
This is a *pivotal time* in human history. A time to rise beyond our fear of otherness. A time to Love with the same radical compassion that Jesus the Christ embodied.

Only when we begin the work of looking within can we grow.
Only then will we heal.
Only then will we **Awake**.

Note on Sources

This book stands on the shoulders of many scholars, clinicians, and theologians whose work has helped illuminate the psychological and spiritual impact of belief systems. It draws on a wide body of interdisciplinary research in psychology, theology, and trauma studies.

Specific works referenced are listed in the References section at the end of the book. Where particular frameworks or ideas originate with others, they are named and credited. Narrative attributions are used where clarity serves the reader; the absence of formal in-text citations reflects the book's intended accessibility rather than a lack of scholarly grounding.

Where interpretation, synthesis, and reflection appear, they arise from the author's own clinical experience and integrative analysis.

All sources are engaged with respect, transparency, and care.

Introduction

I remember being in a field on top of a hill, lying in the soft grass as it cradled and comforted me. I looked up at the beautiful blue sky and knew, *I wasn't alone.*

I was about five or six years old, and even then, I felt a deep connection to something much bigger than myself. This is one of my earliest memories. And as I look back over my life, I can recall many moments like this—reoccurring flashes of **knowing**. A sense that I was connected to something... something beautiful.

LOVE.

I didn't mind being alone or playing by myself. In fact, I preferred it. It was in those quiet moments that I felt the presence of something *other*. A relationship with the Divine was forming, even then.

•••••

I grew up in the rural thumb of Michigan and went to a one-room schoolhouse, which I loved. My siblings—stair-stepped in age, my sister just a year older and my brother a year older than her—would often leave me behind to find my own way home from the fields or trees where we played.

One time, my siblings and I were climbing a tree in our backyard, surrounded by nothing but fields and farmland. At their encouragement, I climbed all the way to the top, and then they left me—just like they often did. I didn't know how to get down, and I have no memory of how I did. But I wasn't scared. No one came for me, but somehow, I found my way—I learned how to follow my instincts... or maybe I was even being guided.

These moments were common in my childhood. And though I never talked about them, they didn't negatively affect my identity. If anything, they taught me to trust myself—to follow my own intuition.

∙ ∙ ● ● ∙ ∙

My mom often told me how much she enjoyed our conversations when I was young. She said I was always "different" in a magical way. She never knew what I would say or how I'd see the world, but she loved the lens I offered. I looked at life from a young age through two lenses: *"I can let this destroy me if I feel sorry for myself"* or *"I can use this to learn and grow."* I have always chosen the latter.

From early on, I had a deep desire to love others—especially those who were the hardest to love.

∙ ∙ ● ● ∙ ∙

In high school, I took an elective called *Introduction to Psychology*, and I knew immediately this was my path. I was fascinated by the human brain and why we do what we do. I enrolled in community college as a first-generation college student, completely unsure of how it all worked. But I ***knew*** something was leading me. So I followed.

One of my early jobs was at a group home for clients diagnosed with schizophrenia. I enjoyed my time there deeply. One resident often invited me on "spaceship rides" to other lands. I never told him it wasn't real—because to him, it was. I simply joined him.

Another resident, a woman, would soften the more I listened to her. When I didn't label her as delusional, she took her medications without resistance, she ate her meals, she let me sit with her. I trusted my intuition.

That job taught me more than any class ever could. I learned how to see people—their *humanity*, their *soul*. I witnessed those who lived in different realities than mine, and I chose to love them.

Eventually, I transferred to a university in Virginia to pursue my bachelor's in psychology. One of my favorite professors was Dr. Captain. A few of us lovingly called him "O Captain! My Captain!"—a reference to the film *Dead Poets Society*. In that movie, one student, Todd Anderson, stands on his desk in protest of his teacher's removal—an act of loyalty, truth, and heart. That scene stayed with me. It stirred something deep inside me, a knowing that I too would one day have to stand for what I believe is **right**. Again, and again, I would have to follow my heart. I would have to trust myself.

Life has a way of challenging you . . .
so that you can remember who you truly are.

⋅⋅⋅•••⋅⋅

My first job after graduation was with the Adult Probation Department, helping felony offenders find employment. I was twenty-two, idealistic, and completely untrained. But I listened. I read case files and chose to see the human behind the history. I saw sons, brothers, fathers—not just "criminals."

That job became a Soul Classroom. It set me on a course I wouldn't fully understand until much later. I showed up with respect. I spoke to them differently than others did. I saw their worth. I *felt* it. I couldn't always explain it to others, but deep inside, I knew: *every life matters*.

That sense led me to a halfway house where I served as a case manager for men transitioning from incarceration. Again, I saw beautiful Souls where others saw statistics. I knew I wasn't better than them—we were connected in a profound way. And I carried a longing from childhood: to *make a difference*.

⋅⋅⋅•••⋅⋅

Eventually, I earned my master's degree in professional counseling and began work as a psychotherapist. In my first role as a psychotherapist, my supervisor held two PhDs and taught me so much, but my greatest teachers were the clients themselves. I ran groups, held space, and listened.

One of my favorite groups met on Friday mornings—a handful of men who had agreed to open our meetings with a spiritual reading of their choosing. It wasn't in the official curriculum, but it was necessary. These men were faithful, vulnerable, and deeply human. We cried together. We laughed. I followed my inner knowing, even when it contradicted my training. And it made a difference.

But something was missing.

Despite using all the skills and best practices I'd learned, the therapy I was trained in wasn't enough. CBT (cognitive behavior therapy) was the gold standard at the time, and I was good at it. But I wasn't seeing the change I longed for in my clients. I began researching trauma—something I had never been formally taught.

That discovery *changed everything.*

I became a trauma specialist and dove into the neuroscience of healing. I followed the voice of intuition once more—and it led me deeper.

• • • • • •

Years later, I moved to California and worked in an agency that served those with state insurance. Many of my clients were homeless, addicted, and carrying deep trauma. I entered yet another level of soul training.

One woman left a lasting imprint. She had been addicted to meth for over 20 years and had lived on the streets for nearly a decade. When she first came to me, she was high, disoriented, and covered in sores. My "training" said to turn her away.

But my soul said: *Love her.*

So I did. I gave her coffee. I listened. I didn't judge her language or her state. And over time... she softened. She began to share her story. She began to trust. One moment I will never forget is when she came to the office with her grocery cart. She started causing a scene outside. She wasn't scheduled to see me that day, but coincidentally I had an opening. So I went out to the parking lot where she was and as soon as I walked outside she ran to me and grabbed me—hugging me tightly. I held onto her for a long time—I held on until *she* let go.

That woman eventually got clean, found housing, reconnected with her children, and began helping her community. Not because I fixed her. But because someone saw her. Because someone offered her *Love*.

She is a person. And all she needed... was **Love**.

· · • • • ·

While all of this was happening, I was working on my doctorate. Every paper I wrote explored trauma, spirituality, and the power of the soul to heal. I fell in love with neuroscience and the mystery of the brain. And when it came time to choose a dissertation topic... I heard a quiet voice.

Spiritual abuse.

At first, I resisted. I didn't want to go there. But I couldn't ignore the knowing. That Still, Small Voice had led me all my life—and it was speaking again. So I said *yes*.

This book, this research, is the result of years of study, but more importantly, of years spent *listening*. Listening to the beautiful Souls who were brave enough to let me hold their pain. This work is about the trauma of spiritual abuse—a wound too often unseen, unnamed, and minimized.

This book is My **Life's Work**. *My* **Heart's Cry**. *My* **Soul's Call**.

May these words bring healing to many.
May your heart be heard.
May your wounds be mended.
May your Soul be restored.
And may you...

Remember Who You Truly Are

PART ONE

Understanding Trauma:
The Impact on the Soul

Part One

There is a quiet truth we carry in our bodies long before we find the words: *Trauma touches everything.*

It does not only arrive as loud, shattering moments. Sometimes, it seeps in slowly—through silence, through systems, through what was never said. Whether born from a single event or the weight of prolonged experiences, trauma is not defined by what happened, but by how it is felt: as harm—physical or emotional—that overwhelms our capacity to cope and leaves us feeling disconnected from safety, from others, from ourselves, and often... from God.

In recent years, the landscape of how we understand trauma has changed. Where we once asked, *"What's wrong with you?"* we now ask, *"What happened to you?"*—a sacred reframe that honors the deeper story and invites tenderness where once there was judgment. This shift has opened new pathways for empathy and healing, reminding us that symptoms are not signs of weakness, but of strength—of a nervous system that has fought to survive.

In medical clinics, educators' classrooms, therapy offices, and spiritual communities, trauma-informed care is slowly becoming the new language of compassion. It is reshaping how we see human behavior—not as brokenness, but as brilliance, as the body's wise response to what it has endured. Professionals across disciplines now turn to research on attachment, the nervous system, and the body to better support healing. And yet...

There is one domain of trauma that still remains largely unspoken.

The wound that comes from the misuse of God.

Spiritual abuse—the distortion of the sacred, often cloaked in righteousness—can be one of the most invisible and devastating forms of trauma. It reaches into the soul's most intimate places. It strikes at the deepest core of who we are and who we believe God to be. To understand this wound, we must begin by understanding trauma not just as a psychological or physical injury, but as a rupture to the soul's knowing.

What follows may stir something deep in you—memories, questions, even grief. Let it. Take your time. Let this be a sacred unfolding. Let curiosity lead. Let compassion hold you.

> This is not just about information, it is about restoration.
> This is about remembering.
> This is about returning to what was never broken in you.

And it begins here, in the stillness of knowing that your pain is real, your story matters, and healing is not only possible—it is your birthright.

Let us begin.

I

Trauma and the Impact on the Self

"Many of us spend our whole lives running from feelings with the mistaken belief that you cannot bear the pain. But you have already born the pain. What you have not done is feel all you are beyond that pain."

—KAHIL GIBRAN

Trauma does not merely touch the mind. It reverberates through the body, the heart, and the soul. Its effects are often hidden, yet profound—shaping the way a person thinks, feels, remembers, and connects to others. When an individual experiences trauma, it is not just an isolated psychological event, it is a holistic rupture.[1] The body remembers. The Soul grieves.

In the field of trauma-informed care, we have seen a powerful shift: from asking *"What's wrong with you?"* to *"What has happened to you?"* This reframing allows compassion to enter the conversation, softening the internalized shame that trauma so often leaves behind.

During my early years working in the adult probation department, in halfway houses, and later as a psychotherapist, I could sense it—something unspoken, something deeper than what the systems and manuals accounted for. These beautiful Souls weren't broken. They were carrying unseen burdens, shaped by pain their nervous systems had never been allowed to process. The missing piece, I came to understand, was trauma. And not just trauma as an event, but as a lasting imprint on the psyche, body, and spirit.

We must never compare or minimize another's pain. Trauma is deeply personal. It isolates. It silences. And it often remains unacknowledged—not because it is insignificant, but because it is overwhelming.

NEUROBIOLOGICAL DEVELOPMENT

Neurobiological development refers to the intricate formation of the brain and nervous system during childhood. Trauma during these formative years can disrupt that process in lasting ways. Neuroscience has begun to uncover just how powerfully early life experiences shape not only the mind, but the architecture of the brain itself.[2,3,4]

Trauma is not just what happened—it is also what happened *inside us* as a result. It affects the wiring of the nervous system. It alters stress responses. And it shapes how we experience safety, trust, and belonging.

Research shows that childhood neglect, abuse, or chronic stress can impair the development of areas in the brain responsible for emotion regulation and memory. The limbic system, particularly the amygdala and hippocampus, is highly sensitive to trauma. The result? Heightened anxiety, emotional dysregulation, anhedonia (the loss of pleasure), and difficulties with attention and memory.[3]

When these brain systems are affected, a person may not even realize how much of their internal world has been shaped by trauma. But understanding how trauma affects the brain brings with it an unexpected gift: compassion. When we understand the "why" behind our struggles, we can begin to soften the harsh self-judgments we carry.

The Limbic System and Emotional Memory

The amygdala acts as our emotional alarm system. It alerts us to danger and governs responses like fear, anger, and anxiety. In trauma survivors, the amygdala can become hyperactive—responding to neutral events as if they were threats. This is why someone may feel perpetually on edge, even in safe environments.

The hippocampus, which helps us form and recall memories, is also impacted by trauma. This region distinguishes past from present, safety from danger. When trauma affects its function, a person may struggle with memory gaps, confusion, or flashbacks. Memories can become fragmented—stored like puzzle pieces instead of coherent stories. As a result, the past may intrude upon the present, uninvited and unresolved.

This is why trauma survivors may feel "stuck" in past events.[5] Their nervous systems are not broken; they are doing exactly what they were wired to do: survive.

But healing is possible. And it begins with understanding.

As you journey through this chapter, I invite you to move gently. If you were neglected, hurt, or dismissed as a child, know that what happened *matters*. Let this knowledge be a lantern—not to relive the pain, but to light a path toward reclaiming your Self.

You are not alone. And you were never meant to carry this alone.

NEUROBIOLOGICAL STRUCTURES AND PROCESSES

Another important area of the brain impacted by trauma is the prefrontal cortex—which, unlike the limbic system, is responsible for higher-order thinking. This region governs decision-making, impulse control, social behavior, and the ability to regulate emotions.[6,7] It acts as the brain's wise guide—helping us pause, reflect, and respond rather than react.

When a person experiences complex or prolonged trauma, the prefrontal cortex can become less active. This means their ability to think clearly, manage emotions, or navigate social situations may be impaired. Simple interactions can feel overwhelming. Trust may be difficult to extend. A person may seem impulsive or withdrawn—not because they lack intelligence or willpower, but because the part of their brain responsible for self-regulation has been affected by pain.[8]

Imagine a child who has been repeatedly harmed or neglected. In a classroom setting, they may lash out at a teacher—not because of the teacher's actions, but because their nervous system has been conditioned to protect them from perceived authority. What looks like "acting out" may actually be a child's nervous system screaming: *I don't feel safe.*

Neurobiological Processes

Understanding how trauma alters the basic processes of brain development brings even more clarity, and *compassion*, to the healing journey. Let's explore four essential neurobiological processes and how they are shaped by experience:

Synaptogenesis, *Formation of Synapses:*

> Synapses are the connections between neurons—tiny bridges where messages pass from one nerve cell to another. In early life, our brains form these connections at a rapid pace, building a complex network for learning, emotion, and memory. When a baby hears a sound or sees a face for the first time, synaptogenesis is taking place. These early interactions literally shape the brain. When trauma occurs, some of these connections can weaken or fail to form, impairing a person's ability to process, regulate, or connect later in life.[9]

Myelinogenesis, *Development of the Myelin Sheath:*

> Neurons send messages more efficiently when their axons are coated in myelin—a fatty substance that insulates and

speeds up transmission. It's like upgrading from dial-up to high-speed internet. Myelin development supports everything from speech to motor control to cognitive clarity. When trauma disrupts this process, the speed and clarity of communication within the brain can be diminished.[9]

Neurogenesis, *Creation of New Neurons:*

Neurogenesis is the generation of new neurons—particularly active in early life and in areas like the hippocampus, which supports learning and memory. While the brain does continue to generate new neurons throughout life, chronic stress and trauma can slow or inhibit this process. This may contribute to difficulties in learning, memory formation, or emotional regulation.[9]

Epigenesis, *Environmental Influence on Gene Expression:*

Epigenesis reveals that our environments don't just affect us emotionally—they actually influence how our genes express themselves. A nurturing, supportive environment may activate genes that promote emotional resilience and brain growth. In contrast, environments marked by fear, neglect, or chaos can "turn on" genetic pathways linked to anxiety, depression, or health struggles. The genes don't change, but how they express does. This is how trauma leaves its mark on the deepest layers of being.[9]

These neurobiological insights are not merely scientific—they are *compassionate lenses.* They allow us to understand that trauma survivors are not broken. They are responding in the only ways their beautifully adaptive nervous systems have known how. And with this understanding, we begin to meet ourselves and others with gentleness, wisdom, and grace.

Neurophysiological Processes and the Power of Connection

Our nervous system is shaped not only by biology, but by relationship. The interactions we have with caregivers in childhood lay the groundwork for how we regulate emotion, connect with others, and respond to stress throughout life. These early attachments form lasting neural pathways, influencing our sense of safety, trust, and self-worth.[7]

Neuroception: The Body's Internal Risk Detector

Neuroception is the autonomic nervous system's subconscious ability to assess whether an environment is safe, dangerous, or life-threatening. This process occurs below the level of conscious thought, relying on subtle cues—tone of voice, facial expression, posture—to guide the nervous system's response.[6,8]

When a child grows up with consistent, attuned caregiving, they develop accurate neuroception. Their body knows when it's safe to relax. Their nervous system learns to remain calm in neutral or supportive environments. For instance, a child who feels emotionally supported at home might enter a classroom and upon hearing a warm voice or seeing a kind face, immediately feel at ease. This sense of safety opens the door to curiosity, play, social engagement, and learning.

Faulty Neuroception: When Safety Cannot Be Felt

But when a child's emotional needs are repeatedly unmet—when caregivers are unpredictable, critical, absent, or unsafe—neuroception becomes impaired. The child's system learns to detect threat everywhere, even where none exists.[6,8]

This is called faulty neuroception. It is not a flaw, but a brilliant survival adaptation. The brain, having learned that safety cannot be trusted, begins to default to protection: *fight, flight, freeze*. The child may become anxious, hypervigilant, or withdrawn. They might react strongly to small stressors, misread neutral expressions as hostile, or struggle to interpret social cues.[6,8]

These protective responses are not defiance or dysfunction. They are the nervous system's attempt to stay alive in a world that has not felt safe.

As the brain develops, these early experiences literally shape its structure. The mind, as neuroscience tells us, *emerges from relationship*. The way we are seen, held, soothed, and responded to wires the circuits that will one day govern our behavior, beliefs, and emotions.[10]

Trauma and the Lens of Perception

A child with faulty neuroception may respond to a neutral classroom as if it were a battlefield. They may lash out at a teacher—not because of that moment, but because of a thousand unmet moments before. What may appear as defiance is, in fact, survival.

I saw this in the eyes of the homeless woman I described in the Introduction. Her nervous system had learned that no space was safe. That no adult was trustworthy. Her abrasiveness wasn't resistance—it was protection. It was the armor her body created to endure a world that had only ever wounded her.

What finally reached her was not a clinical technique—it was *presence*. It was patience. It was love. Her neuroception began to shift not through words, but through consistent safety. When she felt seen without judgment, when my words matched my actions, when she was not rushed or corrected or analyzed... *her nervous system began to soften*.

This is what healing asks of us—not to "fix" others, but to *understand them*. To see beneath the defenses and recognize the Soul that still lives within.

Even in those who seem most hardened, there is still a sacred flicker of innocence. A child within who once longed to be held. When we can offer safety—not just through behavior, but through *embodied compassion*—we give that Soul a reason to trust again.

This is the beginning of healing. And it starts with how we choose to see.

THE STRESS RESPONSE SYSTEM: SURVIVAL OVER CHOICE

Our bodies are designed to protect us. At the core of this design lies the stress response system—an intricate neuromechanism that helps us survive in the face of danger. When the brain senses threat, this system activates automatically, mobilizing the body to fight, flee, or freeze.[11] It does not ask for permission. It does not wait for logic. Its sole purpose is to keep us alive.

This system is miraculous in its design. But when it is overactivated, especially in childhood, it begins to shape a person's inner world not around safety, but around *survival*.

Let's explore the major components that form this protective system:

The SAM Axis: The Body's Acute Alarm System

The SAM axis (sympathetic-adrenal-medullary) is part of the autonomic nervous system's sympathetic branch.[11] It is responsible for our immediate reaction to stress—commonly known as the *fight or flight* response.

When a person perceives danger, the hypothalamus sends a signal to activate the adrenal medulla, prompting the release of adrenaline and noradrenaline. These hormones increase heart rate, blood pressure, and respiration, while funneling energy to the muscles and vital organs.

This response happens in an instant. There is no conscious decision involved—it is the body's way of saying: *Survive first. Think later.*

The Limbic System: The Emotional Interpreter

The limbic system, which includes the amygdala and hippocampus, evaluates the emotional significance of incoming stimuli. The amygdala detects potential danger and initiates the stress response, while the hippocampus processes and stores memories that guide future reactions.

This system bridges emotion and survival. It helps the body remember what hurt, what healed, and what to avoid. When it's shaped by trauma, the limbic system can become hyper-reactive, interpreting everyday experiences as threats.

The HPA Axis: The Long-Term Stress Regulator

For sustained or chronic stress, the body engages the HPA axis (hypothalamic-pituitary-adrenal). This longer-term system begins with the release of CRH (corticotropin-releasing hormone) from the hypothalamus, which signals the pituitary gland to produce ACTH (adrenocorticotropic hormone), ultimately prompting the adrenal glands to release cortisol.[11]

Cortisol helps the body maintain alertness, regulate inflammation, and manage energy usage. But when elevated over time—as in chronic stress or trauma—cortisol becomes toxic. It can impair memory, suppress the immune system, and increase vulnerability to anxiety, depression, and disease.

Trauma's Impact on the Stress System

When a child experiences chronic stress or abuse, these systems are no longer occasional helpers—they become dominant modes of operation.[4,11] The developing brain, flooded with stress hormones, begins to *organize itself around danger*. It wires for survival, not for joy. For vigilance, not for trust.

And here's what's most important: *these responses are automatic.* They are not behavioral "choices." They are the body's instinctive efforts to stay alive.

When someone is stuck in trauma, they may not be able to pause and reflect. They may lash out, shut down, or seem distant. Not because they are choosing to, but because their nervous system no longer believes safety is an option.

This is why we must move away from judgment and toward understanding. Trauma survivors are not broken. They are operating from ancient, sacred systems of protection. When we learn how these systems work, we begin to offer grace. We begin to hold space. And most importantly, we begin to see others not as problems to be solved. But as Souls longing to be safe enough to choose something new.

THE EFFECTS OF EARLY LIFE STRESS ON NEURODEVELOPMENT

According to Dan Siegel, the earliest moments of life lay the foundation for how we experience the world. During the final trimester of pregnancy, the first three years of life, and adolescence, the brain is in a heightened state of development—malleable, vulnerable, and exquisitely responsive to its environment.[10]

When a child experiences consistent attunement, care, and safety during these sensitive windows, healthy patterns of neural connectivity form. These connections shape how the child will regulate emotions, respond to stress, and navigate relationships well into adulthood.

But when early life is marked by neglect, chaos, or trauma, these foundational patterns can be disrupted.

How Early Stress Reshapes the Brain

Early stress can impair synaptogenesis, leading to fewer or weaker connections between neurons—resulting in challenges with learning, memory, and emotional regulation.[11]

It can interfere with myelinogenesis, slowing communication between brain cells—affecting everything from motor coordination to cognitive processing.[11]

It can suppress neurogenesis, reducing the brain's ability to form new neurons—diminishing adaptability and making healing more difficult later in life.[11]

And through epigenesis, early adversity can literally alter how genes are expressed—shaping behaviors, emotional responses, and even physical health for years to come.[11]

Research shows that children exposed to high levels of stress in infancy or before the age of two often show dysregulated stress responses later in life. They may have elevated cortisol levels, heightened anxiety, or an impaired ability to soothe themselves. These effects aren't just emotional, they are physiological.²

The Legacy of Early Imprints

When stress occurs during key developmental periods, it doesn't simply pass through the body and leave. It embeds. It teaches the brain how to feel, how to respond, and what to expect from the world.

These imprints become default settings—automatic patterns that influence how a person thinks, feels, and behaves. A person may grow up believing they are "too sensitive" or "bad at relationships" without ever knowing that their nervous system was wired in response to a lack of safety in their earliest days.

This is why trauma is so often invisible. People blame themselves for their struggles without ever understanding that their brains were shaped by pain long before they had a voice to name it.

Neuroscience as a Path to Compassion

The field of neuroscience is not merely academic—it is revolutionary in the realm of trauma healing. It offers us the insight to see that what feels broken is, in fact, *wounded*. That emotional overreactions are often not overreactions at all, but echoes of an overwhelmed nervous system remembering what it once endured.

This is why, when we find ourselves triggered, flooded, or intensely reactive to a present situation—it is often not the *present* at all. It is the past, surfacing.

It is not weakness. It is memory.

This understanding is what gives us a path forward—not just for healing ourselves, but for responding to others with greater empathy. When we realize that people carry histories written into the architecture of their minds, we begin to soften. We stop asking "*What's wrong with you?*" and begin to wonder, "*What happened to you?*" And in that shift, healing begins.

DEVELOPMENTAL TRAUMA: DISCONNECTING FROM THE SELF TO SURVIVE

Developmental trauma reaches into the very formation of the self. It arises not from a single catastrophic event, but from repeated emotional misattunement, neglect, betrayal, or abuse—especially in the early years, when a child's brain and sense of identity are just beginning to form.[1]

This form of trauma is particularly insidious because it strikes where we are most vulnerable: in our need to be seen, held, and loved. When the caregiver—typically the mother—is unable or unwilling to offer attuned, empathic care, the child begins to adapt in ways that ensure survival, but at the cost of self-connection.

Trauma in the Absence of Safety

Children exposed to chronic emotional abandonment, verbal abuse, betrayal, or violation often develop profound difficulties with emotional regulation, attachment, and identity. When the caregiver's needs consistently overshadow the child's—when the child is used as an object or extension of the adult rather than seen as a subject in their own right—developmental trauma sets in.[1]

The message this trauma conveys is unspoken but deeply encoded: *You are a problem. It would be better if you weren't here.*

To survive, the child learns to disconnect. Not just from the caregiver, but from themselves.

The Brain's Architecture of Attachment

The infant's developing brain organizes itself in response to interaction with the caregiver. The right hemisphere, which governs emotional regulation, undergoes its most significant growth in the first 18 months of life—especially through the process of myelination in the limbic system.[9]

During this time, the child is not learning facts or logic—they are learning *who they are*. And they learn this through mirroring: the way the caregiver reflects the child's emotional states with facial expressions, tone of voice, and gesture.

This nonverbal communication literally wires the brain. Neuroscientists now understand that the *mother's right hemisphere becomes the child's first reality*. The child internalizes her emotional states as their own.[12] When this mirroring is consistent and empathic, the child develops trust, secure attachment, and a coherent sense of self.

But when the caregiver is emotionally unavailable, misattuned, or dismissive, the infant's emotional regulation system is compromised. They may become hyper- or hypo-aroused, unable to manage their internal world. They do not feel safe—not in the world, and not in themselves.

Mirror Neurons and the Need to Be Seen

Mirror neurons, which fire both when we act and when we observe others acting, play a crucial role in emotional attunement. They allow the infant to "feel felt" by their caregiver—to experience their emotions being seen and responded to.

Without this mirroring, the infant does not receive the feedback needed to develop self-awareness. They begin to doubt their feelings, lose trust in their instincts, and construct a *false self* to maintain connection—or simply survive.

The Legacy of Developmental Trauma

Dr. Gabor Maté eloquently writes, "Trauma is not what happens to you. Trauma is what happens inside you as a result of what happened to you." This internal wounding—this rupture of self in the absence of love—shapes the very architecture of the brain.

Children who endure developmental trauma often carry these adaptations into adulthood: dissociation, emotional volatility, self-blame, difficulty forming secure relationships, and a pervasive sense of shame or worthlessness.[12]

And because these patterns are adaptive—they once protected the child from unbearable pain—they are not easily undone.

If You Grew Up Without Safe Love...

If you did not have a safe, loving, emotionally attuned caregiver—particularly in your earliest years—you experienced developmental trauma. This is not said to label or pathologize, but to acknowledge what your nervous system has known all along.

You may have had to disconnect from your true self in order to survive. You may have internalized the belief that *you are a problem* or *you should not exist*.

But here is the truth: *you are not a problem*. You are a Soul who adapted with incredible wisdom. And now, perhaps, you are beginning to remember the deeper truth beneath those early wounds.

You were always worthy of love.
You still are.

COMPLEX TRAUMA: WHEN SURVIVAL BECOMES FRAGMENTATION

Complex trauma is not a single event—it is a chronic condition of the Soul. It stems from prolonged exposure to severe stressors, often during early developmental windows, especially when those stressors are rooted in betrayal, abandonment, or harm inflicted by the very caregivers who were meant to offer safety and love.[12]

When these wounds are repeated and layered over time, the brain adapts not just to survive, but to endure at the cost of connection to the Self.

Dissociation: A Sacred Strategy for Survival

One of the most profound effects of complex trauma is dissociation.[13] This is not merely "spacing out"—it is the brain's biological response to unrelenting helplessness.

When neither fight nor flight is possible, the body chooses a third path: freeze. It enters toxic immobility—a neurological shutdown that muffles sounds, dulls sight, silences voice, and stills the body. In that moment, the brain protects itself by "going inside," turning off the flood of sensory information that could otherwise overwhelm it.

The thalamus, the brain's sensory gateway, can effectively *close the door* to incoming stimuli during acute trauma. This defense mechanism, while adaptive in crisis, can later become a deeply ingrained response—causing people to become emotionally numb or disconnected in everyday situations.[2]

The Long-Term Impact

Over time, repeated use of dissociation as a coping mechanism leads to fragmentation. Not of the mind entirely, but of identity, presence, and emotional coherence. People may feel physically present but emotionally absent. They may be alive, but not fully living.

Research confirms that individuals with histories of complex trauma show distinct patterns of brain function. Neuroimaging reveals altered activity in the limbic system and frontal regions—areas associated with memory, emotional regulation, and self-awareness.[13] These brains are not broken. They are different. They have been shaped by survival.

The Gift Hidden Within

Surprisingly, dissociation is not a flaw. It is a *gift*—a sacred neurobiological strategy designed to protect the Self when nothing else could.

It is a miracle of the human body that in the face of unbearable pain, the mind can create compartments to hold the unholdable. It is not weakness, it is evidence of resilience.

But what protected us then may now keep us from healing. Those who carry complex trauma often find themselves trapped in cycles of self-sabotage, reactivity, or emotional volatility: not because they are unwilling to grow, but because their nervous systems are still whispering: *It is not safe*.

The Path Forward

Understanding complex trauma is not about assigning blame. It is about cultivating compassion—especially for the parts of ourselves that learned to survive in silence, isolation, and fear.

With this knowledge, we can begin to soften. To see our own behaviors not as defects, but as adaptations. To see others through the lens of *"What has happened to you?"* rather than *"What's wrong with you?"*

And most importantly, we can begin to remember what was always true underneath the fear:

You were never the problem.
You were protecting something sacred...
Your *Self*.

And now, with tenderness and time,
You can begin to come home.

CHAPTER 1 SUMMARY
Trauma and the Impact on the Self

Trauma is not just an emotional wound—it is a disruption to the very architecture of the developing brain. At its core, trauma injures the systems responsible for emotional regulation, especially within the limbic system, impairing the mind's ability to process, relate, and feel safe. When early connections with caregivers are absent, inconsistent, or harmful, the foundational ability to form secure attachments—what neuroscience calls neuroception—is interrupted. The result is not just emotional pain, but a miswired nervous system struggling to discern safety from threat.

The brain's most critical developmental processes—synaptogenesis, myelinogenesis, neurogenesis, and epigenesis—are exquisitely sensitive during early childhood and adolescence. These processes are profoundly shaped by one's environment. Supportive, nurturing care strengthens brain development and promotes healthy emotional and cognitive functioning. Chronic trauma, however, especially when left unrecognized or unspoken, leaves lasting imprints that shape how a person learns, relates, feels, and survives.

Developmental trauma, in particular, alters the way a child sees the world, and themselves. The absence of loving attunement from a caregiver deeply impacts the amygdala, hippocampus, and prefrontal cortex, the very regions responsible for memory, emotional regulation, and relational capacity. Children who grow up feeling unseen or unwanted often internalize these messages, forming a distorted sense of self rooted in shame, fear, or unworthiness. These effects are not temporary—they shape the nervous system's response to life itself.

Complex trauma furthers this fragmentation. In the face of repeated violations of safety and trust, the brain's survival mechanisms shift into overdrive. Structures like the thalamus suppress sensory input in a desperate attempt to protect the individual from overwhelm. But this "shutting down" of perception leads to dissociation—a retreat from life, not by choice, but by necessity. Over time, these protective responses become habitual, making it difficult for survivors to feel present, regulate emotions, or connect with others in meaningful ways.

According to Dan Siegel, there are key developmental windows when the brain is most malleable—the last trimester of pregnancy, the first three years of life, and adolescence. Trauma during these windows leaves deep imprints on a person's ability to form healthy relationships and develop a coherent sense of self. The consequence is often disconnection—not only from others, but from one's own inner world.

This chapter invites us into a profound truth: *the way we are shaped is not a matter of weakness, but of adaptation.* When we begin to understand the neurobiological impact of trauma, we stop judging and start healing. And as we cultivate compassion for our own stories, we begin to make space for reconnection—with our Selves, with others, and with the Love that has never stopped trying to reach us.

2

Development of the Self

"I found I had less and less to say, until finally, I became silent, and began to listen. I discovered in the silence, the Voice of God."

—SØREN KIERKEGAARD

Neurologist and professor Dr. Antonio Damasio, a pioneering voice in the fields of neuroscience, psychology, and the study of consciousness, describes the self not as a static identity, but as an evolving process. He proposes that the self unfolds in three interconnected stages: the protoself, the core self, and the autobiographical self.[1]

The protoself is the earliest foundation—a spontaneous mapping of the body's internal state. It arises from the continuous flow of sensory input and bodily signals. In this stage, the self is not yet reflective but is rooted in the lived experience of being—a felt sense of "I exist," emerging from the body's connection to the world. It is the self as object, raw and immediate.

The core self arises in moments of interaction. It is the awareness of the relationship between the body and another object—whether a person, a sound, a sensation. This is where "core consciousness" begins to awaken. It is the experience of here and now, the realization of "I am" in connection to the moment. In this stage, the self becomes the material me, shaped through encounters with the environment.

Finally, the autobiographical self develops through memory and meaning-making. It is the unfolding narrative of who we are, built through layered emotional and social experiences. Damasio emphasizes that the autobiographical self is shaped most profoundly by emotionally rich experiences—particularly those that are spiritual. It is the self as *knower*: the one who remembers, reflects, and anticipates. This is what he refers to as "extended consciousness," and it holds the seeds of soul memory.

But what happens when the world around us is not safe? When emotional, relational, or spiritual trauma is present, the development of the core self can be disrupted. The ability to be fully present, to connect meaningfully with others, and to form a coherent sense of identity becomes fragmented. Without secure relational and spiritual grounding, the formation of the self can be impaired.

In trauma, the world no longer feels mapped or safe. Instead of extended consciousness, we experience constriction. The "knower" becomes hidden beneath layers of fear, shame, and dissociation. And yet, even in the depths of trauma, the Soul remembers. The invitation to return to the self remains.

THE ESSENTIAL ROLE OF SPIRITUALITY IN THE DEVELOPMENT OF THE SELF

Spirituality is not a peripheral element of human development—it is central to the unfolding of the Self. At its core, spirituality invites a sense of meaning, belonging, and connection.[2,3,4,5,6] It offers a sacred ground upon which identity is formed, purpose is shaped, and healing can occur.

Numerous studies show that spirituality and religious beliefs play a profound role in how individuals navigate life's most difficult experiences.[3,7] In the face of suffering, grief, or trauma, many turn inward—to prayer, to reflection, to the sense of something greater than themselves. This inward turn becomes not a retreat from life, but a movement toward integration. Spirituality, when deeply rooted in authenticity rather than dogma, becomes a vital resource for posttraumatic growth.

This truth became evident to me during the years I facilitated the Friday morning After Care group for men in recovery. When we incorporated spiritual reflection—simple, honest engagement with the sacred—these men began to access something within themselves that was deeper than pain, more enduring than shame. Through shared silence, prayer, and soulful conversation, something holy emerged: the resilience of the Soul. Each man, in his own way, was rediscovering that he was more than what had happened to him.

At the heart of the human experience lies a yearning for meaning. This search transcends cognitive frameworks and speaks directly to the soul's desire to remember who it truly is. Dr. Lisa Miller, clinical psychologist and professor at Columbia University, has devoted her life to studying this sacred dimension of the Self. In her book *The Spiritual Child*, she presents compelling research showing that a strong inner spirituality—particularly when self-directed and nurtured in youth—correlates with higher levels of mental health, resilience, and overall well-being.[8]

According to Dr. Miller, in *The Awakened Brain*, spirituality is not about religious adherence or institutional affiliation. It is about a deep, felt sense of connection to a loving presence, a transcendent reality, or the Divine. Her research shows that children with a strong spiritual foundation are more emotionally regulated, have better coping skills, and carry a greater sense of life purpose. This kind of spirituality, unconditional, intrinsic, and Love-based, is protective. It acts as a sacred scaffolding, helping the child grow in strength, trust, and self-awareness.[9]

Equally powerful is the work of neuroscientist Dr. Jill Bolte Taylor. After suffering a stroke that incapacitated her left hemisphere—the center of linear reasoning and egoic identity—Dr. Taylor experienced an overwhelming sense of peace, interconnectedness, and divine unity. Her left-brain functions, including judgment and fear, were silenced. What remained was her right hemisphere's expansive awareness: pure presence, compassion, and a profound sense of oneness with all life.

Taylor's experience underscores something essential. Spirituality is not just a belief system: it is a way of being, a state of consciousness. When the constraints of ego fall away, what emerges is a deeper, more eternal sense of Self. A Self that is not fractured by trauma, not tethered to fear, but radiant, connected, and whole.[10]

This kind of spirituality does not require hierarchy or control. It cannot be imposed. It must be discovered within. And when nurtured, it becomes the very foundation for healing, wholeness, and the sacred return to one's True Self.

THE SPIRITUAL SELF AND THE DEVELOPMENT OF FAITH

Over the past two decades, research has shown that the human mind is intrinsically oriented toward spirituality. Scholars describe this as the "naturalness" of religion—a reflection of the mind's tendency to act, relate, and think in religious and spiritual ways.[4] Developmental psychologist James Fowler supported this understanding, asserting that a partnership with the Divine is a genetically encoded propensity within each of us.[11] Spirituality is not simply a cultural artifact or external tradition; it is a fundamental part of human consciousness. Our beliefs, about ourselves, others, and the world, are deeply shaped by these spiritual inclinations—often operating below the level of conscious awareness.[12]

In this light, we come to see spirituality as central to how we construct our internal world. The Theory of Shattered Assumptions suggests that most individuals carry unconscious beliefs such as: the world is benevolent, people are generally good; the world is meaningful and good things happen to good people; and the self is worthy and capable of influencing outcomes.[3,5] Traumatic experiences, however, challenge these deeply held assumptions. When such beliefs are disrupted, it can prompt a profound internal reckoning—requiring us to reevaluate who we are and what we believe.

This reckoning initiates a process of what is often called a faith change. Typically, it begins with a sense of loss or disillusionment, followed by a deepening of awareness, and ultimately a reclamation of one's own spirituality: a spirituality no longer defined by external doctrines but arising from within.[3] This is the sacred return to the Self. The journey is not away from belief, but toward a more embodied, compassionate, and authentic relationship with the Divine. This is what we come Home to: our Spiritual Self—the sacred, unbroken part of us that holds empathy, compassion, and connection.

To explore this journey further, we must consider the process of psychospiritual development. Just as Piaget outlined cognitive development, Kohlberg mapped moral development, Erikson described psychosocial identity, and Bowlby defined attachment patterns, so too do spiritual theorists invite us to examine the development of the soul. James Fowler's Six Stages of Faith Development has become one of the most influential frameworks in this field.

Fowler proposed that the Self is formed in the context of community, relationship, and meaning-making. Faith is not limited to dogma or belief systems; rather, it is a process of constructing meaning from our lived experience. Through relationships, rituals, language, and culture, individuals move from unconscious participation in inherited beliefs to conscious engagement with their own spiritual truth.[11]

Fowler describes this evolution through three phases: viewing the self as other, viewing the self as self, and ultimately viewing the self in relationship to the Ultimate—God, the Divine, or Source. This movement represents a sacred unfolding. Faith becomes not merely an adherence to tradition, but a lived, evolving journey through belief, devotion, and meaning.[11]

In essence, faith is how we live out our deepest questions... about love, pain, beauty, suffering, and truth. It is the vessel through which our Self comes to know itself and its relationship with the sacred.

STAGES OF FAITH DEVELOPMENT

Primal Faith Stage of Development

Faith begins in the womb. As a child is formed, the emotional environment surrounding the mother—whether expectant and welcoming or anxious and rejecting—becomes the first context of spiritual formation. The moment the child enters the world and takes that first sacred breath, trust or mistrust begins to take root, depending on the environment that greets them. In this stage, there is no distinction between the self and the world. The infant is immersed in pure presence. This stage continues until the development of language begins to differentiate the self from others.

Stage 1. Intuitive-Projective Faith

This stage, most common in early childhood, weaves together imagination and experience. Young children at this age understand the world—and the Divine—through images, feelings, and stories. Faith is not logical; it is intuitive. The emotional tone of religious stories, the behavior of caregivers, and symbols of good and evil are deeply internalized. A loving God might be imagined as a parental figure; a judgmental God, as harsh or distant. The foundation of faith is laid, shaped by the emotional environment more than words.

Stage 2. Mythical-Literal Faith

As a child grows, the world becomes more structured. This stage sees the development of a concrete, literal understanding of religious stories and moral rules. Narrative becomes central to identity—stories about family, faith, and community take root. Right and wrong are clearly defined. God is often viewed as a rule-keeper or moral judge. Abstract symbolism is difficult to grasp at this stage, so beliefs are held in black-and-white terms.

Stage 3. Synthetic-Conventional Faith

This stage brings a capacity for greater abstraction, and is reached in adolescence. Belief becomes more systemic, influenced heavily by key relationships—parents, teachers, religious leaders. There is often a desire to be accepted, to belong. *Faith becomes a social experience.* A strong need to meet expectations from these key relationships and a reliance and dependence on others are essential in the construction of identity and faith. A primary concept of this stage is that of inclusion as an experience of intimacy. How one is experienced and viewed by others is essential to how one views themselves. One's view of God evolves into a more personal, relational one—perhaps a Divine companion who knows us intimately. But this stage is also fragile. The loss of a key relationship can feel like a loss of the self.

Stage 4. Individuative-Reflective Faith

This is the stage of *questioning*. The individual begins to examine the assumptions and beliefs inherited in earlier stages. This can be painful—a deconstruction of faith, identity, and meaning. Authority shifts from external figures to the inner self. One begins to take responsibility for their own beliefs, forming a more authentic worldview. Enhancing one's clarity to transition into individuation—becoming the author of identity and the lifelong journey of becoming who you are. This is the shedding of false identities and integrating all parts of the self—wounded, wise, hidden, and divine. This is a sacred process. It is an awakening to a deeper, more personal connection with the Divine within.

But this new autonomy can give rise to individualism, where connection is forsaken in the pursuit of control. Individualism is the belief that we must do life on our own. Valuing performance over presence, separation over connection. Unlike individuation, which leads to wholeness, individualism can keep us trapped in fear, comparison, and isolation.

Individualism is the illusion of separation. This is a cultural value system that emphasizes independence, self-sufficiency, and personal success above collective well-being or interconnection. While it can promote autonomy and freedom, unchecked individualism often leads to isolation, disconnection, and a sense of spiritual emptiness. This illusion of separateness can distort the truth of our existence—that we are separate from the Divine and even from our own inner being, our Soul. It encourages a performance-based identity—defined by achievements, beliefs, or moral superiority. Rather than a soul-based identity rooted in Love, humility, and relationship.

For those healing from spiritual abuse, this often shows up as pressure to have the "right" answer, to prove one's worthiness, or to perform righteously in order to be accepted.

Where Individuation moves us toward integration and authenticity. Individualism can keep us trapped in self-judgment, comparison, and fear. Healing requires recognizing that we were never meant to journey alone. True wholeness comes from connection… with the Self, with others, and with the Divine Love that binds us all.

Individuation is the psychological and spiritual process described by Carl Jung as the journey of becoming the truest version of oneself. Becoming whole doesn't come through achievement or perfection, but through integrating the fragmented parts of the self. The hidden places within the unconscious, the shadow, and the wounded inner world—this is where the sacred unfolding begins. It is the gradual discovery and embodiment of one's unique essence—the Soul's fingerprint. One is able to disentangle from societal roles, religious expectations, and internalized beliefs that no longer serve them. Moving from survival into authenticity, from conditioning into freedom.

For those healing from spiritual abuse… This is not a rebellion, it is a resurrection. One begins to live no longer from fear or conformity, but from inner alignment and Love. They become rooted in their inner truth—the Divine core within. A homecoming to the Soul.

Few ever reach this stage before young adulthood, if reached at all.

This stage, while important, is not the final destination.

Stage 5. Conjunctive Faith

Here, the ego softens. One begins to see that the self is made of many selves, and that truth often comes in paradox. There is a growing openness to mystery, a reverence for the sacred held within story and symbol. One becomes more compassionate, more spacious in how they hold difference. *Intimacy is no longer about control—it becomes about presence.* In this stage, the soul listens more than it speaks. One has developed the capacity to stay open and no longer hold on to rigid beliefs with religious mindsets; one is able to have conversations with others that hold different opinions and beliefs while still holding onto one's own beliefs. There is a yearning to follow the Spirit's guidance, and a capacity to wait, to seek, to surrender. Few ever reach this level before middle adulthood, if reached at all.

Stage 6. Universalizing Faith

This is the rarest and most radiant stage. Here, one is no longer centered in the self, but grounded fully in the Divine. This stage is marked by transformation: a unitive consciousness where the heart, the mind, and the soul are aligned with Love. The self is no longer the subject of faith, God is. The individual becomes a vessel of Divine compassion, justice, and grace. These souls—like St. Francis or Martin Luther King Jr.—live with radical courage, *embodying Love without conditions.* A truly transformational process has taken place in this stage. This person is a type of ambassador of the Kingdom of God. They do not just believe in the Divine—they become a living reflection of the Divine.

·· • • • ··

Faith is a journey through all aspects of our humanity—biological, emotional, cognitive, spiritual. Fowler's stages offer a map, not a mandate. They help us understand that questioning, struggling, and evolving are not signs of failure, but signs of growth.

Why does this matter?

Because the 'Spiritual Me'—the deepest, truest part of the Self—is rarely cultivated in our modern world. We are trained to identify with the 'Material Me'—our job, our looks, our roles, our performance. But beneath all of that is the Soul. The part of you that cannot be earned, bought, or broken.

You are a Beautiful Soul, who is Deeply Loved.

Ask yourself:

> Do I love without condition?
>
> Do I embrace those different from me—not as projects, but as friends?
>
> Can I hold space for beliefs that are not my own?

If not, perhaps there are more stages ahead of you. . .

This is not a race. *It is a becoming.*

CHAPTER 2 SUMMARY
The Development of the Self and Stages of Faith

Dr. Antonio Damasio, a neurologist and professor, proposes that the construction of the Self unfolds in progressive stages, culminating in the formation of the Spiritual Self. According to his work, this final dimension arises from social and emotional experiences—particularly those that are spiritual in nature. These experiences provide a framework of meaning, grounding the individual in connection, belonging, and self-awareness. When the natural development of these stages is disrupted by trauma or stress, it can impair the healthy construction of the Self, leading to confusion, disconnection, and fragmentation.

Dr. Jill Bolte Taylor, a neuroscientist who experienced a transformative stroke, offers a profound insight into the relationship between brain function and spirituality. Her unique perspective highlights the right hemisphere's role in spiritual awareness and a felt sense of interconnectedness. She describes moments of stillness, presence, and unity as essential to emotional and psychological health, reminding us that transcendent experiences are not abstract—they are neurologically real.

Dr. Lisa Miller, a clinical psychologist and pioneering researcher, has shown through empirical research that spirituality, especially when nurtured in childhood, acts as a protective force for emotional and psychological well-being. Her studies affirm that spirituality is an innate part of the human condition, serving as a vital source of resilience, meaning, and inner strength across the lifespan.

Dr. James Fowler, a developmental psychologist and theologian, offered a foundational framework for understanding psychospiritual development through his Theory of Faith Development. His model outlines six stages of faith, with the final three being particularly transformative for the formation of the Self.

Stage Four invites the individual into individuation, where they become the author of their own beliefs, values, and identity—stepping into a more authentic version of themselves. This stage is a critical stage of change. One can move *into the beauty of individuation* or be driven into individualism.

Stage Five opens the soul to paradox and complexity, welcoming new interpretations of truth, and allowing for intimacy *without* control, beliefs *without* rigidity, and love *without* fear. The ego softens, and one begins to listen for the movement of Spirit.

Stage Six, the rarest and most sacred, is a complete decentration from the egoic self. The individual no longer lives from a constructed identity, but instead from union with the Divine. This is not self-denial—it is *Self-fulfillment*. It is the discovery of the True Self, rooted not in achievement or appearance, but in sacred participation with God's love.

Together, the research of these scholars reveals that our psychological and spiritual development are inseparably intertwined. To understand the self fully, we must also honor the spiritual journey each soul is invited to walk. This path leads us inward—through growth, rupture, and reformation—until we rediscover what was always true:

We are made for Love, and we are already held by it.

Part One Summary

Understanding Trauma:
The Impact on the Soul

A vast body of research has shown that trauma deeply impacts every area of a person's life—mind, body, and soul. In recent decades, neuroscience has revolutionized our understanding of this impact, offering unprecedented insight into how trauma is encoded in the brain and body. We are in the midst of a cultural awakening—a Zeitgeist moment—where trauma is no longer viewed solely through the lens of pathology but as a holistic disruption that calls for a holistic approach. Yet, one area remains largely underexplored: how trauma affects the Spiritual Self.

Trauma disrupts emotional regulation in the brain's limbic system, injuring not only the mind but also one's capacity for connection and inner peace. Dr. Dan Siegel explains that trauma interrupts healthy attachment formation by impairing neuroception—the brain's ability to detect safety—which begins in the earliest phases of development. Crucial neurodevelopmental windows such as the last trimester of pregnancy, early childhood, and adolescence lay the groundwork for relational well-being and emotional resilience. When these processes are disrupted, the individual's connection to Self is also impaired.

Severe and repeated trauma—particularly developmental or complex trauma—can cause the brain's thalamus to shut down, fragmenting sensory processing and emotional integration. This leads to dissociation, a neurobiological response to overwhelming threat in which the mind disconnects to preserve survival. Though protective, these adaptations can impair long-term well-being, relational capacity, and a person's ability to access their inner world.

Dr. Antonio Damasio suggests that the Self is not something we are born with fully formed—it is constructed over time through social experience. Most profoundly, he asserts that spiritual experiences play a defining role in shaping our sense of identity. The final stage of self-construction, he proposes, is the emergence of the Spiritual Self—a stage that is too often stunted or neglected in Western culture.

Dr. Lisa Miller's groundbreaking research brings scientific validation to the protective power of spirituality. She shows that individuals with a strong spiritual core exhibit greater resilience, emotional regulation, and neural pathways associated with healing and hope. In *The Awakened Brain*, Miller presents spirituality not merely as belief, but as an innate capacity of the human brain to perceive a greater reality—one that fosters recovery and emotional thriving. Her work is particularly powerful in the context of spiritual abuse, as it demonstrates that authentic spirituality can be a pathway to healing, not harm.

Dr. Jill Bolte Taylor, a neuroscientist who experienced a profound stroke, offers another lens through which to understand spiritual awareness. Her left-brain shutdown allowed her to experience the world through the right hemisphere alone—giving her a felt sense of unity, stillness, and Divine connection. Her journey revealed that spiritual experiences are not simply poetic, they are neurobiological realities. Taylor's insight invites us to value quietness, stillness, and the deep knowing that lives beyond logic.

Authentic spirituality cannot be imposed. It must be discovered. A vital part of spiritual development is the freedom to explore one's beliefs through personal experience and reflection, rather than through external pressure or control.

Dr. James Fowler's Theory of Faith Development maps the inner terrain of this journey. He proposes that faith evolves in stages—moving from inherited beliefs to a deeply internalized, embodied spirituality. The final three stages are pivotal in the construction of the Spiritual Self.

Stage Four is the path of individuation. Here, a person begins to question previously held assumptions, ultimately becoming the author of their own life and beliefs. It is not an easy path—it involves the disintegration of inherited identities so that new, authentic wholeness can emerge.

Individuation is the inner work of returning to the core of who we truly are. It is the re-membering of our fragmented selves. A rejoining. A becoming.

Stage Five is the transition from rigidity to openness. The ego, once necessary for protection, begins to soften. One recognizes that faith is not about control, but about freedom. This stage allows for paradox, for mystery, for spiritual intimacy that does not demand conformity.

Stage Six, the Universalizing Stage, is exceedingly rare but profoundly beautiful. In this final stage, the self is no longer the center of awareness. The person becomes rooted in the Divine. Their thoughts, actions, and presence flow from Love itself. They have become a living expression of the Kingdom of God—compassionate, transcendent, and free.

This section reminds us of a powerful truth:

We are not just bodies.
We are not just thoughts.
We are Souls on a journey to *Remember Who We Truly Are*.

PART TWO

Unveiling the Wound:
How Evangelicalism Harms the Soul

Part Two

We have explored the profound impact of trauma on neurodevelopment, as well as the sacred role of spiritual formation in shaping identity. Now, we turn to one of the most hidden and painful subjects in this field of study: the psychological and spiritual consequences of *spiritual abuse*. This section is not intended to attack those who adhere to religious beliefs or practices, but rather to shine a compassionate light on how certain teachings and systems, when rigid or misused, can become toxic. The goal is not to tear down faith, but to illuminate a path of healing for those whose sacred connection to the Divine has been distorted or damaged.

This is a gentle invitation to remember who you are. To reclaim the voice within. To restore your soul's sacred knowing: *You are a Beautiful Soul, Deeply Loved.*

When I was discerning the topic of my dissertation and felt the unrelenting call to research spiritual abuse, you may wonder: *Why this?* After more than a decade specializing in trauma—working with individuals who had endured profound grief, abandonment, violence, and betrayal—I thought I had seen the depths of human suffering. And yet, a pattern began to emerge that left me unsettled. I started to see clients whose symptoms mirrored complex trauma—emotional dysregulation, shame, fear, disconnection from self—but there was no obvious traumatic event in their history.

What they *did* have in common was this: at one point in their lives, they had all been part of a religious community.

It was then I began to ask deeper questions. Could teachings wrapped in the language of God, salvation, and righteousness be silently wounding people's sense of self? Could these symptoms of despair, anxiety, and shame be the result of teachings that told them they were inherently sinful, unworthy, or untrustworthy?

This form of trauma—the spiritual kind—is the most elusive, the most devastating, and, tragically, the most dismissed.

It is what compelled me to spend the next three years immersed in research, collecting stories, analyzing patterns, and seeking clarity about this particular form of harm that lives in the shadows. What I discovered confirmed what I had felt in my Soul for years: *spiritual abuse is real*, and it reaches into the deepest places of a person's psyche—because it affects their view of God, of Love, of Belonging, of Self.

Let me be clear: this research is not a condemnation of faith or religion. On the contrary, it is a defense of true, sacred spirituality. The kind of spirituality that nourishes the soul, fosters intimacy with the Divine, and honors the dignity of every human being.

I know there are communities of faith that offer safety, freedom, and unconditional love. If you are part of such a space—one that supports spiritual growth without coercion, encourages curiosity rather than conformity, and honors the sacred autonomy of each soul—I honor you. Thank you for being a light.

But for those who have been harmed by fear-based theology, rigid doctrine, spiritual manipulation, or shame-driven teachings—this part of the book is for you.

I do not blame those who perpetuate these teachings; often, they too are repeating what they were taught. But we must begin to tell the truth. We must speak aloud the harm. And we must begin the sacred work of healing.

If you have found yourself questioning your worth because of a sermon, silencing your intuition to remain "obedient," or living in fear that you are never "good enough" for God—may this be the beginning of your homecoming.

To the heart of Love. To your inner sanctuary. To the Sacred Self that was never lost, only hidden.

Welcome to Part II.

3

Abuse in Christian Religion

"There are two ways to be fooled. One is to believe what isn't true; the other is to refuse to believe what is true."

—SØREN KIERKEGAARD

The Christian Church, throughout its history, has not only provided spiritual guidance and community but also, tragically, been a source of spiritual abuse and religious intolerance. Historical accounts reveal a long shadow of persecution, holy wars, inquisitions, and witch hunts—all carried out in the name of religion. To understand the depth and the pernicious nature of spiritual abuse today, we must be willing to embrace the Zeitgeist—the spirit of the times—and also bravely peer into the painful legacies of our past.

E.G. Boring, president of the American Psychological Association in 1928, wisely proposed the importance of the Zeitgeist in shaping ideas. He reminded us that no idea is formed in a vacuum; for a new idea to take root, the cultural environment must be ready to receive it.[1]

We are now living through such a moment.

The Deconstruction of Faith movement within American evangelicalism has become one of the most significant cultural shifts in modern religious life. It signals a collective awakening—a refusal to stay silent any longer about the harm perpetuated in the name of God. If we dare to pay attention, we will recognize this moment for what it is: a call to finally name, confront, and heal the long-ignored trauma of spiritual abuse.

May we be brave enough to ask the hard questions.

May we open our hearts to the painful truths of those who have suffered.

May we rise as a generation that no longer turns away but instead, sets the captives *free*.

Isn't this the very message Jesus embodied?

Isn't this the radical Love He came to reveal?

WHAT IS SPIRITUAL ABUSE?

Spiritual abuse occurs when harm is inflicted in the context of one's spiritual or religious life—often at the hands of leaders or fellow believers who misuse spiritual authority. It can manifest as manipulation, coercion, intimidation, or control. Over time, these dynamics corrode a person's autonomy, self-trust, sense of worth, and their relationship with the Divine.[2,3]

This form of abuse is pernicious—its effects are often subtle at first, creeping in gradually until the harm becomes entrenched in the person's psyche and soul. It dismantles one's ability to think freely, relate openly, or connect safely with oneself, others, or the Sacred.

Though often linked to cultic or fringe groups, spiritual abuse also occurs within mainstream religious traditions, including evangelical Christianity, when authority is distorted and used to dominate rather than serve.

The wounds left by spiritual abuse are not merely emotional or intellectual.

They are *existential*.

They cut into the deepest places of trust, identity, and belonging.

Spiritual abuse has long remained unnamed—hidden beneath religious language, shame, or the assumption that questioning spiritual authority equates to rebellion or sin. But it is now being recognized as a legitimate and devastating form of trauma. In clinical literature, it is beginning to be categorized not only as psychological injury, but as a *psychospiritual wound*—one that often remains invisible even to those experiencing it.

THE SILENT SUFFERING OF SOULS

Victims of spiritual abuse often suffer in silence, unsure how to articulate their pain—let alone identify it as trauma. Because the abuse is wrapped in spiritual language or done "in the name of God," many blame themselves for feeling confused, anxious, or disoriented.

Some leave their religious communities altogether, not out of a loss of faith, but out of a desperate need to survive.

Studies show that over the last decade, there has been a rapid decline in individuals identifying as Christian. Of those who have left, a significant percentage once belonged to fundamentalist or evangelical communities. Research reveals that many of these departures are not driven by a loss of belief in God, but by toxic church environments that foster control, guilt, and spiritual suffocation.[4]

They are leaving to breathe.

They are leaving to remember who they truly are.

HISTORY OF RELIGIOUS ATROCITIES

Spiritual abuse is still an underrepresented topic in the field of psychology, yet its influence stretches across nearly every era of human history. From the brutal persecution of Christians in the Roman Empire under Nero in 64 CE—where simply identifying as a follower of Jesus was punishable by death for nearly three centuries— through the Crusades (1095–1258), the Roman Catholic Inquisition of the 12th century, and into the late Middle Ages where practicing any faith outside of Catholicism became perilous, religion has long been entangled with power, control, and violence.

The Protestant Reformation, while sparking significant reform, also fueled persecution and gave rise to the infamous 17th-century witch hunts which resulted in the deaths of nearly 80,000 individuals, many of whom were brutally executed in the name of religious purity.[5]

Spiritual abuse, then, is not new. It is woven into the cultural and religious fabric of our history.

While this book does not attempt to catalog the full extent of atrocities committed in the name of God, it is important to acknowledge this legacy. Religious leaders have at times wielded spiritual authority to justify unthinkable cruelty—acts of dehumanization that were not only allowed but sanctified under the guise of devotion.

Our focus here is on a more insidious and contemporary form of spiritual abuse—one that is subtle, systemic, and deeply embedded within evangelical and fundamentalist Christian subcultures today. It does not wear the robes of Crusaders or the banners of inquisitors, but it leaves no less of a wound. In many ways, its covert nature makes it even more damaging.

THE DECONSTRUCTION OF FAITH MOVEMENT

The fastest-growing non-religious group in Western society today is composed of those who are not abandoning faith itself, but escaping the spiritual abuse they endured within religious institutions.[6] This phenomenon is often described as deconversion, or more commonly, as the Deconstruction of Faith Movement.[7]

In this context, deconstruction refers to the process by which individuals begin to critically examine and unravel the belief systems, doctrines, traditions, and ideologies they were taught—often for the first time in their lives. Rather than being a rejection of faith, it is more often a courageous and necessary stage of spiritual evolution. This is the beginning of the Fourth Stage of Faith Development – Individuative-Reflective Faith.

Yet within the evangelical community, deconstruction is rarely seen this way. It is viewed as dangerous. Rebellious. Even demonic.[8,9]

Those who embark on this path are often met with shaming tactics—labeled as *heretics*, *backsliders*, or accused of being under satanic influence. They are ostracized, dismissed, and emotionally exiled from their faith communities. The very people who once embraced them now turn away. The result is a profound loss of social support and a deep psychological rupture—creating intense loneliness, confusion, and grief.[4,6]

Evangelicalism, as a subculture, often leaves little room for nuance or questioning. Its belief system is non-negotiable. Its theology is rigid. Its answers are final. The unspoken rule is clear: this is the one true way and anything else is false, dangerous, and leads to eternal damnation.[7,10,11,12]

And so, many who leave the evangelical church do not only lose their community: they also face the terrifying possibility that they have lost their salvation. The psychological toll of this indoctrinated fear cannot be overstated.

THE SPARK THAT IGNITED THE MOVEMENT

One of the earliest and most visible sparks of the modern Deconstruction of Faith Movement came in 2011, when well-known evangelical pastor Rob Bell published his book *Love Wins*. In it, he dared to question key doctrines of evangelicalism, including eternal damnation, original sin, and the exclusivity of salvation. Bell was immediately labeled a *false teacher* by other prominent evangelical leaders and effectively exiled from the inner circles of evangelicalism.[10,11]

But something profound began to stir.

In 2016, two former evangelicals, John Williamson and Adam Narloch, launched *The Deconstructionists Podcast*. Their honest, open conversations created a safe space for listeners to wrestle with their own faith questions—without fear or shame. The podcast became a sanctuary for many and has since released over 234 episodes, helping to usher in what they describe as a *new reformation* among disillusioned evangelicals.[10]

That same year, Blake Chastain, another former evangelical, launched the *Exvangelical Podcast*, offering support for others navigating their departure from the church.[12] Chastain's podcast, with 230 episodes, has over 800,000 downloads. He partnered with Chris Stroop, who helped launch a social media movement using hashtags like #Exvangelical and #EmptyThePews—calling for mass exodus and collective healing. At the time of this writing, the hashtag #Exvangelical has been used over 875 million times.

The term *Exvangelical* has since become a recognized social movement with its own Wikipedia entry. A private Facebook group by the same name has grown to over 13,000 members and counting.

In 2017, YouTubers Rhett and Link, hosts of *Good Mythical Morning*, shared their personal stories of leaving the evangelical church—an episode that garnered over 1.6 million views and thousands of comments from viewers experiencing similar awakenings.

Since then, faith deconstruction has surged across social media. Entire platforms, podcasts, and communities now exist to support those on the journey of spiritual disentanglement. Instagram pages, Facebook groups, TikTok, and podcasts like *Nomad* - "Stumbling through the post-Christendom wilderness, looking for signs of hope" offer connection and solidarity to those navigating this sacred unraveling.[11]

What began as isolated whispers has become a growing, collective voice.

This movement is not about abandoning faith.

It is about rediscovering it—outside of fear, shame, and control.

It is about remembering how to listen to your own soul.

It is about coming Home.

THE EMERGING CHURCH

At this juncture, scholarly literature within the social sciences on the Deconstruction of Faith Movement remains almost entirely absent. While academic attention has begun to observe a related movement known as the *Emerging Church*, little has been formally documented about the more widespread and urgent wave of spiritual departure now occurring—particularly within the subculture of conservative evangelicalism and fundamentalist Christianity in the United States.

Anthropological fieldwork conducted between 2007 and 2011 identified the *Emerging Church* as a cultural shift—a grassroots response to the megachurch model and the rigid systems of religious thought and political alignment characteristic of the Religious Right.[13] This movement does not have a central figurehead or institutional structure. Instead, it was catalyzed by individuals seeking a more authentic, compassionate, and inclusive expression of Christian spirituality—one free from the judgmental and hierarchical frameworks they had experienced within evangelicalism. This movement is not marked by rebellion.[13,14]

Historically, religious reformations have often stemmed from a longing for spiritual transformation—a return to purity, humility, and the heart of the gospel of Jesus. The *Emerging Church* appears to be comprised of those who are in opposition of conventional Christianity, signifying a transition of religious orientation.[15]

What is striking, and perhaps even unprecedented, is that according to the research available, no previous movement in Christian history has produced such widespread deconstruction from the core tenets of the faith itself.[16,17,18] This is not merely a denominational shift. It is a profound *existential reckoning*. For many, it has led not just to leaving the church, but to walking away from Christianity entirely.

And yet, the social sciences remain largely silent.

There are few, if any, peer-reviewed studies examining the psychological, emotional, and spiritual impact of this exodus. Very little has been published on the harm inflicted by the ideologies of evangelicalism—on how deeply they wound the psyche, distort identity, and sever the innate connection between soul and Spirit.

And so I offer this truth:

This is why I did this work.

As a clinical psychologist and trauma specialist, I embarked on a phenomenological study because I could no longer ignore what I was witnessing in my practice. Brave souls, many of whom carried no visible scars from what we traditionally define as trauma, were showing signs of deep suffering: anxiety, dissociation, shame, spiritual despair. And one by one, I began to see the thread that bound them.

They had all, in some way, been wounded by the Church.

There was no diagnosis for it. No formal literature to cite. No established treatment protocol. But I *knew* what I was seeing. And I *knew* what I was feeling. This was not a rebellion against God—this was grief. This was not apostasy—this was soul injury.

At the time of this writing, I have found no scientific research dedicated specifically to understanding the psychological and spiritual harm caused by evangelicalism as a religious system. The silence in academia only adds to the silencing many have already experienced in their churches.

And so, I broke the silence.

This work—the study, the writing, the deep listening—was born out of a need to tell the truth. To give language to what has been endured in silence. To witness the wounds of those who were told their suffering was "rebellion" or "lack of faith"—when in truth, it was evidence of a soul refusing to be buried by shame.

This research does not seek to attack religion. It seeks to *liberate* spirituality from the systems that have distorted it.

It seeks to offer a way back to the Sacred.

It is time we see this for what it is. Not as rebellion, but as revelation.

Not as destruction, but as *awakening*.

HISTORY OF AMERICAN EVANGELICALISM

To understand the present-day culture and teachings of evangelicalism, we must begin with its origins—because most who belong to this denominational structure have never been taught how it began. They have inherited beliefs, rituals, and dogmas without ever asking the vital question: *Where did this come from?* For many, the assumption is that the teachings of evangelicalism originated directly from Jesus or the early apostles. But history tells a different story: one that is necessary to revisit if we are to understand the roots of modern spiritual trauma.

Sociologists and scholars of religious history point to a 19th-century figure, John Nelson Darby, as a central architect of what would become modern evangelicalism and Christian fundamentalism in the United States. Darby, an Anglo-Irish clergyman and founder of the *Plymouth Brethren* movement, introduced a radically new interpretation of Scripture that formed the basis for dispensationalism—a theological framework that divided history into "dispensations" or separate eras of God's interaction with humanity.[18,19,20]

This ideology introduced, for the first time in Christian history, a detailed theory of *premillennial eschatology*—focusing on apocalyptic "end times" prophecies and a belief in the sudden disappearance of believers in what Darby called the *rapture*. According to Darby's vision, Christ's return would happen in two phases: first, a secret rapture in which the faithful would be taken up to Heaven before a period of tribulation, and second, a public return of Christ to establish a thousand-year reign on earth. Prior to this teaching, no Christian tradition (Orthodox, Catholic, or Protestant) had ever embraced such a view. It was, in truth, a theological invention of the 1830s.[20,21]

What began in small separatist circles in Ireland and England would soon find its way to American soil.

Following the societal devastation of the Civil War and World War I, many Americans were drawn to a theology that offered comfort, control, and a hopeful escape from suffering. This is where Cyrus Ingerson Scofield—a Civil War veteran, lawyer, and later theologian—played a pivotal role in embedding Darby's teachings into the heart of American religious culture.[21]

In 1909, Scofield published the *Scofield Reference Bible*, an annotated version of the King James Bible that included his personal commentary interwoven with the biblical text. This version was revolutionary. Not because of the text itself, but because it framed the Scriptures through the lens of dispensational theology. For the first time, Darby's eschatological views were accessible to the masses, packaged as part of the biblical canon itself. The influence of the *Scofield Bible* cannot be overstated—it became a foundational text for many evangelical churches and Bible colleges, profoundly shaping American Christian thought for generations.[21,22]

What is often overlooked, however, is the human story beneath this theology.

Both Darby and Scofield experienced personal traumas that likely influenced their theological developments. Darby, following the untimely death of his mother at a young age and disillusionment with institutional religion, withdrew into a separatist spiritual worldview that sought refuge in a future heavenly escape. Scofield, having endured moral failings, legal troubles, and personal breakdown, found redemption and stability in a system that emphasized spiritual order, judgment, and the certainty of salvation for the elect. Their theology was not birthed in peace—it was shaped by pain.

As Dr. Marie T. Hoffman—psychologist, psychoanalyst, and researcher—proposes, the roots of modern evangelicalism were not merely intellectual; they were *trauma-informed*. Dr. Hoffman's work explores how 20th-century American evangelicalism was not only built upon doctrinal shifts, but upon the unresolved personal and collective trauma of its founders. The belief systems they created offered control, predictability, and rigid moral structure as a way to soothe the deeper existential fear and loss they carried.[23,24]

But these systems did not heal trauma—they transferred it.

And over time, these beliefs were passed down as absolute truth, leaving little room for spiritual curiosity, emotional expression, or psychological development. The legacy of dispensationalism became more than just theological, it became cultural. A subculture emerged that privileged certainty over mystery, hierarchy over autonomy, and judgment over compassion.

It is essential to understand that these beliefs were not inevitable. They were constructed, shaped by individual pain and historical context, and then institutionalized into something that many now believe is inseparable from Christianity itself.

But it is not.

And perhaps this is the most liberating truth of all: *What has been constructed can also be deconstructed.* What has caused harm can be reevaluated in the light of Love. And what was once rooted in fear can be transformed through the sacred process of healing and spiritual maturation.

John Nelson Darby (1800–1882)

John Nelson Darby was born into a wealthy Anglo-Irish family in London in 1800. Raised amid privilege and refinement, Darby's early life afforded him the education and opportunity that would prepare him for a career in law or the Church of England. Yet despite his promising beginnings, Darby became increasingly disillusioned with the institutional structures and spiritual complacency he witnessed in the established Church. What began as restlessness grew into a deep inner rupture—a longing for something more authentic, more alive, and more aligned with the purity of Scripture.

This yearning led him to separate from the Church of England and become a founding figure of what would later be known as the *Plymouth Brethren* movement. The Brethren emphasized simplicity of worship, the sole authority of Scripture, and a conscious separation from ecclesiastical hierarchies. Darby believed that the institutional Church had drifted too far from its spiritual roots—and he longed to return to a purer, more direct connection with the Divine.[20,22,25]

A pivotal moment in Darby's spiritual transformation occurred in 1827 when he suffered a serious riding accident. During his long convalescence, Darby entered into a deep period of introspection, theological reflection, and personal revelation. It was during this vulnerable season of solitude that Darby began to formulate the theological framework that would later become known as dispensationalism—a system that would go on to radically shape evangelical thought across continents and generations.[20,22,25]

Darby proposed that God works in distinct eras, or "dispensations," each marked by a specific mode of divine governance and human responsibility. At the heart of his eschatology was a newly articulated belief: the *pre-tribulational rapture*. This view held that faithful believers would be "caught up" to meet Christ prior to a seven-year period of tribulation on earth, followed by Christ's millennial reign. This concept—now familiar in many evangelical churches—was revolutionary at the time. No Christian tradition before Darby had ever systematized such a view.[20,22,25]

Darby's interpretive lens was rigidly literal, especially regarding prophetic and apocalyptic texts. He believed that the Bible, when read systematically and free from human tradition, revealed God's ultimate plan for history in exacting detail. In his own words, Darby once wrote, *"I did not learn my theology from books, nor from professors. I received it directly from the Word of God."*[26] This statement reveals the heart of his conviction—and the deep individualism that defined his theological approach.

Yet while Darby framed his theology as purely biblical, it is clear that his personal experiences profoundly influenced his worldview. His break from ecclesiastical institutions, his physical vulnerability following his accident, and his spiritual longing for order and divine clarity all converged in the theological system he would go on to share with the world.

It is essential to acknowledge both the intellectual and emotional origins of Darby's work. What may have begun as a sincere desire for spiritual purity became, over time, a rigid framework that emphasized separation, divine judgment, and apocalyptic expectation. The theology Darby introduced would eventually lay the foundation for a powerful subculture, modern evangelicalism, particularly in the United States.

Darby's impact is enduring. Through his writings, teachings, and influence on figures like C.I. Scofield, his ideas were seeded into the soil of American religious life. But we must also examine the fruit of that seed. For all its structure and prophetic certainty, Darby's dispensationalism often created fear rather than freedom, dogma rather than depth, and spiritual division rather than divine intimacy.

As we begin to unravel the history and harm of American evangelical theology, we must begin here—with a man who sought the purity of faith, but whose theology would eventually be used to build the very structures of rigidity and exclusion he once sought to escape.

Cyrus Ingerson Scofield (1843-1921)

C.I. Scofield, one of the most influential figures in American evangelical history, is best remembered for editing the *Scofield Reference Bible*—a publication that profoundly shaped 20th-century dispensational thought and left an indelible mark on American Christianity. While his theological contributions are often studied through the lens of eschatology and biblical prophecy, a closer look at Scofield's life reveals a more complex story—one marked by personal turbulence, redemption, and the deep longing for divine order amidst human chaos.

Scofield's early years were marked by instability. He served briefly during the Civil War but found his postwar life in disarray. His marriage to Almeda, his first wife, ended in abandonment. He left her and their two daughters—an act that carried both emotional and social consequences. He also became embroiled in legal and financial scandals, including forgery and questionable business dealings, which resulted in a stint in jail. These events fractured his reputation and cast a shadow over his early adulthood.[21,22,27]

But in 1879, a pivotal transformation occurred. Amidst personal ruin, Scofield experienced a dramatic evangelical conversion. This moment of spiritual awakening marked a turning point—one in which he redirected his life toward ministry, biblical study, and the pursuit of theological clarity. It was not just a turning of the page—it was, for Scofield, the writing of an entirely new chapter. From the ashes of his former life, he emerged with a fervent belief in the inerrancy of Scripture and a deep commitment to a theological vision that promised redemption, structure, and divine intervention.

He embraced dispensationalism (a theology first articulated by John Nelson Darby) which divides history into distinct periods or "dispensations" in which God interacts with humanity in different ways. This framework, emphasizing the literal return of Christ, the rapture of the Church, and the millennial reign, provided Scofield a structured lens through which to view the chaos of both his inner and outer world. In an era scarred by the trauma of war, industrial revolution, and cultural fragmentation, this vision of history offered both explanation and hope. For many, it was a divine roadmap—assuring that justice would prevail, suffering had a purpose, and the faithful would be rescued.

In 1909, Scofield published the first edition of *The Scofield Reference Bible*. This groundbreaking work included study notes, cross-references, and theological commentary that codified his dispensational views. For many readers, it became more than a Bible—it became a theological compass, guiding how Scripture was read, understood, and lived. His work helped institutionalize pre-tribulational rapture theology, shaping seminaries, churches, and generations of evangelical believers across the United States.[21,22,27]

Though it is speculative to draw direct psychological parallels, many scholars have noted how Scofield's personal history—marked by instability, guilt, and failure—may have profoundly influenced his theological vision. His deep longing for divine order, justice, and separation from worldly chaos mirrors a soul that had once known disorder, shame, and collapse. In this way, his theology became not only doctrine but balm—a structured belief system that offered clarity where life had once offered confusion.

C.I. Scofield's legacy endures. His theological framework continues to inform many strands of evangelical teaching, especially within communities still shaped by dispensationalist thought. But beyond his doctrines lies a deeper truth: that theology often arises from the deepest parts of our humanity. His story reminds us that belief is never formed in isolation. It is born from wounds, longing, redemption, and the hope that what is broken might one day be made whole.

Dwight Lyman Moody (1837–1899)

Dwight L. Moody was one of the most influential figures in American religious history. He was a tireless revivalist, founder of the Moody Bible Institute, and a man whose passion for evangelism touched the lives of millions. His name became synonymous with the spiritual awakenings of the 19th century, yet his legacy is complex. While Moody's ministry was rooted in a deep desire to bring souls to Christ through love, he also played a significant role in popularizing dispensational theology—a theological framework that, while offering clarity and urgency, often ushered fear into the spiritual imagination of generations to come.[27]

Moody's early ministry reflected the revivalist culture of his day—emphasizing sin, judgment, and the need for salvation. His sermons painted a stark picture of humanity's fallenness and the impending danger of eternal separation from God. Like many of his contemporaries, he believed that stirring the heart through fear could awaken repentance. Yet something shifted in him. One evening, Moody listened as the evangelist Henry Moorehouse preached on John 3:16 for an entire week. Each night, Moorehouse spoke not of wrath, but of God's radical Love. The message pierced Moody's heart. He later described it as a moment of profound awakening—one that transformed the way he preached and understood God's heart.[27]

From that moment, Moody began to emphasize Love over fear. His sermons still called for repentance, but they now rested more deeply in the assurance of God's grace. He spoke of a tender Savior who longed to embrace the wounded, the weary, and the searching. His shift was not just theological—it was personal. He began to see faith not merely as escape from judgment, but as an invitation into healing relationship with the Divine.

Yet even as Moody's heart was expanding toward Love, he became one of the primary American voices to elevate and spread dispensationalism—a theological system introduced to him by members of the Plymouth Brethren and shaped by John Nelson Darby's eschatology. This framework, which divided history into divine "dispensations," offered a compelling and ordered narrative of human destiny. It highlighted a pre-tribulational rapture, a seven-year tribulation, and a final apocalyptic reckoning.[21,22,28]

Though Moody never formally systematized these teachings himself, he lent his considerable influence to those who did. Through his preaching networks, publishing endeavors, and the founding of the Moody Bible Institute in 1886, he helped embed dispensational theology into the heart of American evangelical education. Through his endorsement and the momentum of his institutions, the teachings of Darby—and later, C.I. Scofield—gained theological legitimacy and cultural traction.

This blend of heartfelt revivalism and eschatological urgency formed a potent spiritual climate. While Moody personally experienced a shift toward Love, the system he helped promote often re-centered fear: fear of judgment, fear of being left behind, fear of never being good enough. For many, salvation came to feel conditional and precarious—tethered to the looming vision of end-times catastrophe.

Moody's legacy is therefore layered. He was a man of profound conviction and compassion, one who opened hearts to the tender grace of God. And yet, in amplifying dispensationalism, he also helped construct a theological scaffolding that would later be used to justify rigid belief systems, exclusionary practices, and spiritual fear. The gospel he once softened with Love was, for many, reshaped into a system of urgency and dread.

Still, Moody's story is not one of contradiction, it is one of complexity. Like so many reformers and revivalists, his life held both beauty and unintended consequence. He reminds us that theology is never neutral—it reflects the soul of its messenger. And it calls us to remain vigilant and tender in how we speak of God, for the stories we tell about the Divine shape not only doctrine but the lives, and wounds, of those who hear them.

DISPENSATIONALISM AND THE FRAGMENTATION OF FAITH

Dispensationalism is a theological framework that divides human history into distinct eras, or "dispensations," in which God interacts with humanity in different ways. At its core is a literal interpretation of Scripture and a belief that each dispensation begins with a divine blessing and ends with human failure, resulting in judgment. The culmination of this system is the rapture: the sudden removal of believers from the world, followed by a time of tribulation and divine reckoning.[20,21,28,29]

This eschatological narrative, *introduced* by John Nelson Darby, *systematized* by C.I. Scofield, and *popularized* by D.L. Moody, shifted the spiritual imagination of generations.

What was once a gospel of redemption and restoration became, for many, a message centered on fear, urgency, and escape. Rather than anchoring the believer in a present moment infused with divine presence, dispensationalism pointed toward an imminent departure—a future deliverance that eclipsed the importance of living with integrity and compassion in the here and now.

This framework ushered in a profound theological shift: from a faith grounded in healing love and sacred presence to one preoccupied with punishment, separation, and survival.

ABUSE WITHIN EVANGELICALISM

The psychological and spiritual consequences of this shift are staggering. Dispensational theology contributed to what Dr. Marie T. Hoffman identifies as three primary fractures within evangelicalism—horizontal, vertical, and temporal splits—each carrying distinct wounds to the soul.[23,24,30]

The Horizontal Split

This rupture is the division between the sacred and the secular, between spirituality and the lived reality of human suffering. In the early 1900s, evangelicalism moved away from the ethical emphasis of the Holiness Movement—personal sanctification expressed through care and justice—and toward a highly individualized, experiential spirituality. This inward focus encouraged believers to bypass the pain of the world and retreat into a private faith insulated from suffering.

The result was a spiritual narcissism that prized emotional experience over embodied compassion. Pain, injustice, and systemic suffering were often spiritualized away or ignored altogether. Those struggling within the community were encouraged to "claim victory" and suppress their distress, lest they appear spiritually deficient.

The Vertical Split

Here, the fracture lies between the earthly and the heavenly—the "us" and "them." Faith was no longer a means of communion but a means of categorization. Evangelicalism began to portray the world as enemy territory: those within the fold were saved; those outside were damned.

This dualistic worldview bred fear, judgment, and religious superiority. The gospel became militant, marked by "muscular Christianity," a stoic, hard-edged version of faith where vulnerability was weakness and emotional struggle a spiritual failure. Evangelicals were taught to prioritize soul-winning over soul-listening, conversion over compassion. Those in pain were often sidelined unless their suffering could be packaged into a testimony of triumph.

The Temporal Split

Finally, the temporal divide distorted how believers saw time itself. Rather than embodying the love of Christ in the present—caring for the sick, feeding the hungry, welcoming the stranger—dispensationalism encouraged escape. This world was not our home. The future was all that mattered.

Hope was no longer placed in the unfolding of God's love here on earth, but in a dramatic departure from it. Suffering was no longer something to transform but something to outlast—endure until rapture. This theology led to widespread emotional dissociation: a disengagement from the present moment, from personal suffering, from the cry of the neighbor, and ultimately from the True Self.

•••••••

Dispensationalism—though framed as divine truth—introduced a fracture in the soul of the Church. It suppressed grief, shamed doubt, dehumanized suffering, and presented a version of God more concerned with separation than intimacy. The trauma caused by this theology is not metaphorical—it is real. And it runs deep.

This form of harm is spiritual abuse. It is subtle, systemic, and often unrecognized even by those who experience it. It severs a person from their own inner knowing, from their sacred right to question, to feel, to evolve. It creates a false self that conforms out of fear and represses the truth of one's soul in order to belong.

But at the heart of all true spirituality is the journey back—back to the God who is *Love*, back to the soul who was never lost, only buried. Spiritual abuse does not have the final word. There is another path.

In the words of Jesus the Christ:

> *"Great sorrow awaits you religious scholars and you Pharisees—such frauds and pretenders! You do all you can to keep people from experiencing the reality of Heaven's Kingdom realm. Not only do you refuse to enter in, you also forbid anyone else from entering."*
>
> —MATTHEW 23:13, *The Passion Translation*

Let these words echo not as condemnation, but as a call. A call to unmask the systems that harm. A call to return to the Sacred Love that was never about fear, and never about earning. A call to remember who we truly are.

BELIEFS OF AMERICAN EVANGELICALS

In my research "evangelical" is defined using the NAE LifeWay Research Evangelical Beliefs Research Definition based on their own research and proposed definition as stated below. This is taken directly from their website at www.nae.org:

> The National Association of Evangelicals (NAE) initiated the development of an evangelical beliefs research definition for accurate and consistent use

among researchers. In partnership with LifeWay Research the definition was crafted, reviewed and tested for validity.

On October 15, 2015, the NAE Board of Directors adopted the evangelical research definition.

The NAE/LifeWay Research evangelical beliefs research definition uses four questions to measure evangelical beliefs.

Respondents are asked their level of agreement with four separate statements using a four-point, forced choice scale (strongly agree, somewhat agree, somewhat disagree, strongly disagree). Those who strongly agree with all four statements will be categorized as evangelical:

- The Bible is the highest authority for what I believe.
- It is very important for me personally to encourage non-Christians to trust Jesus Christ as their Savior.
- Jesus Christ's death on the cross is the only sacrifice that could remove the penalty of my sin.
- Only those who trust in Jesus Christ alone as their Savior receive God's free gift of eternal salvation.

The tab from the website titled *Statement of Faith* states:

We believe the Bible to be the inspired, the only infallible, authoritative Word of God.

We believe that there is one God, eternally existent in three persons: Father, Son and Holy Spirit.

We believe in the deity of our Lord Jesus Christ, in His virgin birth, in His sinless life, in His miracles, in His vicarious and atoning death through His shed blood, in His bodily resurrection, in His ascension to the right hand of the Father, and in His personal return in power and glory.

We believe that for the salvation of lost and sinful people, regeneration by the Holy Spirit is absolutely essential.

We believe in the present ministry of the Holy Spirit by whose indwelling the Christian is enabled to live a godly life.

We believe in the resurrection of both the saved and the lost; they that are saved unto the resurrection of life and they that are lost unto the resurrection of damnation.

We believe in the spiritual unity of believers in our Lord Jesus Christ.

Additionally on the website under the tab *What is an Evangelical?* It states:

> Our community brings together Reformed, Holiness, Anabaptist, Pentecostal, Charismatic and other traditions. As noted in the statement "Evangelicals — Shared Faith in Broad Diversity," our core theological convictions provide unity in the midst of our diversity. The NAE Statement of Faith offers a standard for these evangelical convictions.
>
> Historian David Bebbington also provides a helpful summary of evangelical distinctives, identifying four primary characteristics of evangelicalism:

CONVERSIONISM
>the belief that lives need to be transformed through a "born-again" experience and a lifelong process of following Jesus.

BIBLICISM
>a high regard for and obedience to the Bible as the ultimate authority.

ACTIVISM
>the expression and demonstration of the gospel in missionary and social reform efforts.

CRUCICENTRISM
>a stress on the sacrifice of Jesus Christ on the cross as making possible the redemption of humanity.

>These distinctives and theological convictions define us—not political, social or cultural trends. In fact, many evangelicals rarely use the term "evangelical" to describe themselves, focusing simply on the core convictions of the triune God, the Bible, faith, Jesus, salvation, evangelism and discipleship.

Evangelicals currently comprise nearly twenty-five percent of the American population, making them the largest religious group in the nation.[23, 24, 30] Social scientists increasingly recognize evangelicalism as a distinct subculture within the broader religious landscape—one that often thrives on conflict as a means of reinforcing exclusivity, rigid moral codes, and tightly held doctrinal positions.[31] Within this framework, belief is not merely a matter of faith but of compliance. The dualistic, dogmatic nature of evangelical teaching leaves little room for spiritual autonomy or individual exploration. For many, this creates a sense of captivity rather than connection—where personal freedom, critical thought, and the natural unfolding of one's spiritual journey are constrained by the fear of judgment or exclusion.

CHAPTER 3 SUMMARY
Abuse in Christian Religion

A profound movement is unfolding within evangelicalism—the Deconstruction of Faith movement—now recognized as the fastest growing non-religious shift in Western society. Never before in modern Christian history has such a sweeping departure from the core tenets of faith been recorded, as millions step away from institutional religion in pursuit of personal spiritual integrity.

This mass exodus did not emerge from irreverence, but rather from the deep and cumulative impact of theological systems that, for many, no longer resonate with their evolving understanding of God, humanity, or Love. Central to this shift is the theological legacy of John Nelson Darby and C.I. Scofield—two men whose personal pain, disillusionment, and need for order helped shape the dispensationalist framework that now permeates much of modern evangelicalism. Their emphasis on the rapture, divine judgment, and prophetic timelines offered a sense of certainty and control amid the chaos of their lives. But these teachings, rooted in trauma, birthed a system more focused on escape than engagement, fear rather than freedom.

Though early Christian texts speak of a future return of Christ, the systematic theology of a pre-tribulation rapture (as articulated by Darby in the 1830s) was a novel development. Scofield's 1909 annotated Bible ensured its widespread adoption, embedding this eschatology into American evangelical consciousness for generations. What began as a theological lens soon became a cultural identity, tightly woven into evangelical doctrine and discipleship.

Yet this framework has come at a cost.

Evangelicalism, as a subculture, often thrives on control—reinforced through rigid beliefs, exclusive moral codes, and an unwavering claim to spiritual authority. As Dr. Marie T. Hoffman has noted, this theological structure has inflicted traumatic wounds, leading many into dissociation—psychological and spiritual fragmentation that results when suffering is suppressed, invalidated, or ignored.

The damage is not merely doctrinal. It is psychospiritual.

This form of spiritual abuse—covert, systemic, and often unrecognized—reaches into the soul. It obstructs the sacred journey of self-discovery and disrupts the unfolding of faith into its more mature, integrated forms. It denies the possibility of union with the Divine through Love and instead replaces it with fear, conformity, and the suppression of questions.

But now, a threshold has been crossed. The movement away from these harmful ideologies is not an abandonment of faith—but a return to its essence.

It is the Soul remembering who it truly is:

A Beautiful Soul, Deeply Loved.

4

Spiritual Abuse: Wounding the Immortal Soul

"You don't have a soul. You are a Soul. You have a body."

—C.S. LEWIS

From the ancient wisdom of philosophers to the cutting-edge findings of neuroscience, a profound truth continues to emerge: the Soul—the deepest essence of who we are—is immortal, sacred, and whole.

Plato's reminiscence theory of knowledge teaches that the Soul existed before entering the body and that learning is, in essence, *remembering*. For him, the supreme aim of life was not merely intellectual development, but liberation—freeing the Soul from illusions to awaken its true nature. Aristotle echoed this reverence, teaching that the Soul gives life its very form and holds within it the innate capacity to grow into its fullest expression. Philo, merging Greek philosophy with Jewish mysticism, described the Soul as a fragment of the Divine—a sacred breath of God carried within every human being.[1]

Modern neuroscience, far from contradicting these ancient perspectives, brings them into new light. Dr. Antonio Damasio, renowned neurologist and professor, affirms that the Self is not a separate entity from the body or mind, but a seamless integration. The Soul, he suggests, is not an abstract concept but a lived, neurophysiological reality. It is the essence of our Being—subjective, undivided, and immeasurably unique.[2]

Scientific studies exploring the neurological basis of religious experience have uncovered what researchers refer to as the "God center" in the brain. Neuroimaging has shown that spiritual experiences are not merely intellectual beliefs, but embodied emotional states. They are not just thoughts; they are *thinking that feels like something*.[3] This intertwining of emotion, trust, and belief reveals that our encounters with the Divine are as deeply felt as they are understood—and that they are shaped by both biology and culture.

Perhaps most significantly, the pioneering work of Dr. Lisa Miller reveals that spirituality is not a passive trait or a learned behavior—it is a core part of human neurobiology. Through her research, she proposes that we each possess what she calls *the awakened brain*—an innate capacity to connect with a greater spiritual reality. Her studies show that this spiritual orientation is a protective factor against mental suffering, depression, and despair. It enhances resilience, fosters emotional clarity, and strengthens our capacity for love and meaning.[4]

As Dr. Miller writes, "Whether or not we identify as religious or spiritual, our brain has a natural inclination toward and docking station for spiritual awareness. The awakened brain is the neural circuitry that allows us to see the world more fully and thus enhance our individual, societal, and global well-being."[4]

This understanding reaffirms what ancient sages have long known: the Soul is not peripheral, it is central. It is not metaphor, it is essence.

And so we must now confront a truth long hidden in the shadows: *spiritual abuse is a trauma that violates the Soul*. Unlike other forms of harm, it strikes at the immortal core of our Being. It distorts one's sacred connection to the Divine. It dismantles trust, silences intuition, and severs the deepest parts of the Self from the sacred ground of Love.

This is not a wound of mere belief, it is a wound of *Being*.
Spiritual abuse cannot be minimized. It cannot be brushed aside as theological disagreement or religious immaturity. Its harm is profound, its consequences far-reaching—and for many, it leaves the deepest scars of all. Because it does not merely confuse the mind or frighten the heart. *It violates the very place where we experience the Divine.*
And that is why this must be named.
That is why this work is sacred.
And that is why your healing is Holy.

SPIRITUAL ABUSE AND RELIGIOUS TRAUMA

Spiritual abuse is a unique and deeply wounding form of trauma. It occurs within the sacred space where trust in the Divine is meant to reside—and instead, that space is manipulated, violated, or distorted by individuals wielding spiritual authority. This form of harm inflicts a kind of suffering that no other abuse can replicate, because it touches the most intimate parts of the human experience—our longing to be connected to something greater, to be loved unconditionally, and to know that our Soul is safe.

When spiritual abuse occurs, the violation is not just emotional or psychological, it is sacred. It leaves behind a wound that many describe as *soul murder*—a severing of the heart's deepest trust in Love, in God, and often in themselves.[5,6,7,8,9,10]

Dr. Marlene Winell, a psychologist who pioneered this area of study, coined the term Religious Trauma Syndrome to describe the cluster of symptoms experienced by individuals leaving rigid, authoritarian, and fundamentalist religious systems.[7] These systems, such as those found in many evangelical communities, are often structured around control—using fear, guilt, and manipulation to enforce compliance.

Dr. Winell's research reveals how teachings from these communities—particularly those that misuse sacred Scripture or claim absolute authority—can cause profound psychological distress.

Spiritual trauma is more than coercion; it's indoctrination. It replaces inner knowing with fear, silences doubt with shame, and often leaves individuals deeply fragmented from their truest Self.

Dr. D.W. Winnicott's concept of the *false self* offers a powerful lens for understanding this trauma. In communities where only one way of being, believing, or behaving is acceptable, children and adults alike may feel they must abandon their true feelings and thoughts to belong. Over time, they construct a version of themselves that complies with the system, all while the authentic self retreats into hiding.[6] This disconnection from one's own voice, needs, and intuition is not only psychologically damaging, it is spiritually devastating.

TOXIC THEOLOGY

Certain theological teachings, particularly those rooted in fear, have the power to wound the Soul. Beliefs that center around Divine punishment, eternal damnation, or inherent human depravity often instill chronic guilt, shame, and self-loathing. Over time, these teachings do not simply shape beliefs, they shape *identity*.[11]

The doctrine of biblical inerrancy, for example, discourages questioning and intellectual exploration. In many evangelical spaces, even voicing doubt or wrestling with Scripture is seen as a threat. Those who ask difficult questions are often shamed, silenced, or excluded. This fosters a culture of spiritual control—where loyalty to doctrine is equated with loyalty to God, and where fear masquerades as faith.

It's important to acknowledge: these doctrines do not represent the whole of Christianity. Many denominations within the broader Christian tradition reject literalism, dualism, and punitive theology. There are faith communities centered in grace, mystery, and compassion. But it is the authoritarian, absolutist expressions of evangelicalism that often produce spiritual trauma—and these are the focus of this chapter.

DAMAGING DOCTRINES

Eternal Damnation

The teaching of eternal torment in hell has been used to terrify generations into submission. Graphic descriptions of the "lake of fire" and the "gnashing of teeth" are not simply theological metaphors—they become psychological strongholds.[7] For many, the fear of being forever separated from God creates a chronic state of inner panic. This fear doesn't motivate love—it generates a life-long struggle to be "good enough" to escape punishment. In doing so, it fosters dissociation from the parts of the self that are human, tender, and imperfect.[6,12]

Substitutionary Atonement

The belief that God required the violent death of His own Son to satisfy divine wrath—and that our salvation hinges on accepting this sacrifice—can be deeply traumatic. While this doctrine is central to many evangelical teachings, it also paints a portrait of a wrathful God who demands blood to forgive. This vision distorts the nature of Love. It can lead people to believe that they are fundamentally unworthy unless someone else suffers in their place. The psychological toll is immense: it creates a cycle of guilt, perfectionism, and fear of losing salvation. Individuals often live with anxiety over whether their "conversion" was real enough, deep enough, sincere enough—and whether they've done enough to stay saved.[6,12]

Original Sin

The teaching that every human is born in sin and separated from God reinforces the belief that something is inherently wrong with you. From the earliest age, individuals are taught that their desires cannot be trusted, their hearts are deceitful, and that they are inherently broken. This leads to deep self-alienation and impedes the natural psychological development of trust in oneself.[6,12] In parenting, this belief can be used to justify harsh discipline and emotional manipulation, framing it as "God's will" for breaking a child's sinful nature. The result is often trauma masked as obedience.[11]

Evangelizing and Witnessing

Evangelicals are taught they must save others from eternal torment. This burden can feel crushing. If a loved one dies without converting, they are believed to be in hell. The result is profound grief, guilt, and spiritual anxiety—particularly for children raised with this belief, who carry the weight of others' "salvation" as their personal responsibility.

Dispensational Eschatology

The belief in the rapture—that "true believers" will suddenly disappear while others suffer horrific tribulation—has deeply affected the evangelical imagination. Children are often traumatized by the fear of being left behind. The founder of this theology, John Nelson Darby, taught that human suffering is unworthy of attention—that true believers must focus on Heaven and not be "distracted" by earthly pain. This promotes emotional repression, spiritual bypassing, and a disconnection from human suffering. The dualistic worldview it fosters—good vs. evil, saved vs. lost, spiritual vs. earthly—leads to dissociation from one's own body, emotions, and lived experiences.[13]

•••••

These teachings do not just shape ideas.
　They *shape lives*.
　They influence how people view themselves, relate to others, and understand God. They produce *existential trauma*—a rupture at the core of identity, purpose, and belonging. They cause people to

question whether they are lovable, worthy, or even real. They lead to a fractured inner world where doubt is sin, sadness is weakness, and suffering is proof that something is wrong with you.

And this is the heartbreak: the very spaces that should offer sanctuary become sites of trauma. The very teachings that claim to lead to life end up severing people from their own aliveness. This is why spiritual abuse must be named. It must be understood as more than theological disagreement—it is a sacred wound to the Soul.

And no Soul deserves to be harmed in the name of God.

LIVED EXPERIENCES OF SPIRITUAL ABUSE

In my phenomenological study, ten courageous participants from across the United States—ranging in age from 24 to 57—shared their lived experiences of spiritual abuse within evangelical Christian communities. These individuals represented diverse regions, with 8 women and 2 men from ten different cities and eight different states. Their educational backgrounds ranged from high school diplomas to graduate degrees, including one participant currently in seminary and another who had formerly served as a pastor within the evangelical system.

Each participant had been immersed in evangelical communities for a significant portion of their lives, ranging from 7 to 41 years. Two remained actively involved in their communities at the time of their interviews. The remaining eight had left their churches, having been away for periods ranging from one week to twenty years. All ten identified having experienced spiritual abuse within these systems. To verify this, each participant completed the Spiritual Harm & Abuse Scale (SHAS), which confirmed their qualification for this study.[14]

Using Heidegger's hermeneutic phenomenology, I examined the patterns that emerged from their testimonies through careful thematic analysis. Initial codes surfaced, such as "control/manipulation," "pressure to perform," "spiritual hierarchy," "judgment and shame/doubt," "mental health as spiritual weakness," "biblical literalism," and "no room for humanity." These codes evolved into five overarching themes:

1. Religious Indoctrination
2. Cognitive Dissonance
3. Spiritual Bypassing
4. Emotional Dissociation / Disconnection from Self
5. Disenfranchised Grief

In the following pages, you will hear the direct voices of the participants (no names are used to preserve their anonymity and dignity). Their words are untouched, raw, and profoundly brave.

As you read, I invite you to take tender care of your own Soul. You may find that their stories stir memories or emotions from your own spiritual journey. Please move through this section slowly. Pause when needed. Breathe. Reach out to trusted supports or professional guidance if anything surfaces that feels overwhelming. Let yourself be held as you bear witness to theirs.

THEME ONE:
Religious Indoctrination

Religious indoctrination, as described in this study, is the use of psychological manipulation within a spiritual context to achieve obedience, conformity, and unquestioned loyalty to a group's values, doctrines, and hierarchical authority.[15] At its core, it is a disruption of the natural unfolding of an individual's consciousness. It severs autonomy and rewires the psyche to submit—often under the guise of spiritual maturity.

The purpose of indoctrination is not transformation but control, not illumination but silence. This silence is the suppression of doubt, of emotion, of questioning, and ultimately of Self. It demands obedience, not through informed belief, but through pressure, fear, and survival-based compliance.[15] In many evangelical communities, the goal is not spiritual maturity, but uniformity—an unquestioning loyalty to the group's theology and values.

When this type of indoctrination is enacted in the name of God, it doesn't just shape thoughts, it alters identity. It creates a rift between the individual and their inner knowing, separating them from the Self and from their own sacred autonomy.

All ten participants in this study spoke to this experience. Their stories echo with recurring patterns of control, spiritual hierarchy, suppression of emotion, exclusion, shame, and a forced submission to authority. Each participant in this study shared the oppressive reality of this control.

Submission was not presented as a sacred practice of humility but a mandated surrender of one's will and voice. "You had to submit, even if you don't agree. Submit even if you're not sure." This demand often targeted women and those considered spiritually "weaker," imposing roles cloaked in righteousness but rooted in suppression. "A lot of pressure to submit. I felt this pressure to be this submissive wife and Christian and you had to do it joyfully—so you don't even get to be angry about it. You want to please God and do the very best you could. A lot of control happens to just really sincere people just wanting to be good."

A deeply embedded power structure further reinforced these systems of obedience. Pastors and church leaders were portrayed as spiritual authorities whose directives could not be questioned without spiritual consequence. "A lot of control with anyone with power. There's unwritten rules that made it very evident that that's what you are supposed to do. Whatever the Pastor says, or leaders, say is it. If you didn't follow you would not be rewarded with positions... you would feel shame for not doing what they said we were supposed to do... you wouldn't be in the 'in crowd'... you wouldn't be favored—the interactions would be difficult." Spiritual favoritism, conditional belonging, and social exclusion became tools of discipline. "If you didn't [attend all the services], you didn't get invited to things... you know people looked down on you."

Performance, not presence, became the currency of belonging. "If I'm not doing anything... then I'm not as worthy of the relationship... it's like a prerequisite of being respected." The moment one questioned a doctrine or challenged the norm, they were shunned—silently or overtly. "Membership is big in evangelicalism. If you question any of the beliefs you can't be part of the church... social exclusion is implied, you get excluded." Even difference of thought carried the weight of shame. "There is this 'otherness' if you disagree... this judgment and feelings of shame if you had different opinions."

These teachings were not limited to behavior—they shaped entire worldviews. They fostered animosity toward outsiders and deep distrust of alternative beliefs or traditions. "Anyone who is not a believer is wrong and you can't trust what they are saying... you just have to only look at this perspective of being 'Christian.'" This dichotomous, black-and-white worldview disrupted natural developmental processes of self-reflection, critical thinking, and empathy. The result was a system that prohibited individual thought and moral complexity—hallmarks of spiritual maturity.

Sexuality was particularly weaponized. Participants recounted how purity culture and teachings around sinfulness entrenched shame and self-rejection, particularly toward those who identified as LGBTQ.

> "Sex was supposed to only be between a man and a woman and only if you are married... Homosexuality and pre-marital sex were considered to be sin." "The church I attended believed they were progressive on this because they didn't believe you had a choice. So, the language they used was something like 'some people have heavier crosses to bear than others.' So, if you're gay, the cross you're being asked to bear is the cross of celibacy. I shared with my mentor that I was struggling with same-sex attraction and her response was that she no longer wanted me around her children because I would be exposing them to sin."

Some were told that even being around LGBTQ individuals was dangerous.

> "I personally was told that I couldn't have dinner with someone in that community or talk with them."

"We were very homophobic. So, like if you're gay, you can't act on that—that's a sin. Anything like sex outside of marriage, you have to wait until marriage. You can't live with anyone until you're married either, that's a sin. You are not allowed to date someone who is not a Christian, that's also a sin."

The pressure to suppress one's authentic self in favor of conformity left many feeling monstrous for their natural desires. "Always feeling like a monster who's trying really hard to be a knight. I look back now and the very idea that the word purity to me means sex. . . man! The idea was to shut off anything regards to sex completely. If you crossed that boundary of purity you would be impure."

Homosexuality was viewed not as identity, but as a symptom of brokenness. "Homosexuality is a defect created from harm—you were damaged so that's how this came about."

At the core of this belief system was a narrative of total depravity—that every individual is inherently evil and worthy of judgment. "You are taught that you are unworthy—you are a sinner." The constant message was: "You're bad, God's mad, try harder. . . You are born already so effaced by original sin that you have no capacity to please God. I was striving to make sure I didn't become worthless." One participant summed it devastatingly well:

> "The framework or theology is that your heart is deceitful above all things and you're wicked and totally depraved. The gospel is 'We are more horrible than we could ever imagine, but we are loved more than we could ever conceive.' So, there is nothing good in us. The reason Jesus died was so that when God looks at us He doesn't see our shitty, awful, self. He sees how good Jesus is. So basically, you turn off anything that's bodily about you, you turn off your emotions, your intuitions, you turn off your gut. You are stripped of any kind of control or humanity. . . it's the turning off of what you know in your gut to be true."

This indoctrination created a kind of learned helplessness, a spiritual paralysis. The message was consistent: *You cannot be trusted. Your heart is deceitful. Your feelings are suspect. Your questions are dangerous.*

Biblical literalism became a barrier to growth, curiosity, and intellectual freedom.

> "There's no room for the Bible to be flawed, no room at all. . . which is fucking insane and makes me angry to the point that—I would cry about it if I let myself. That is the one thing that caused so much harm, Christians don't allow for questioning scripture—you aren't allowed to challenge it. If you disagree. . . it's just not okay to disagree—as if only one interpretation exists. If you question it you're going to get some form of punishment back."

To question the Bible was to be ostracized, to be seen as rebellious or spiritually immature.

Leadership was revered as divinely appointed, beyond reproach.

> "The Word of God is inerrant, and every word is God-breathed and meant to be taken literally. You aren't allowed to question. What the Pastor says is law. If you question you are ostracized."

> "It's not safe to question or disagree."

> "I was held back because I was taught that the Bible was literal. They would say 'so when you are in biology class they are lying to you. . . it isn't true.' A lot of indoctrination—you don't know at the time. You can't doubt whether this religion is true because if you doubt—well maybe you're not saved and you're on your way to Hell. It was terrifying.

This created a toxic dynamic in which questioning leaders was equated with disobedience to God. This enforces an external locus of control, stripping individuals of their inner compass.

Participants described "Christianese"—the coded language of their communities—as a way of reinforcing groupthink and avoiding vulnerability. "If their humanity peeks out, that's called the 'flesh' and that's not a good thing." Words like "rebellion," "flesh," "demonic attack," and "sin nature" became tools to pathologize natural emotional responses. "In Bible college the Dean of Women said to me 'that was rebellious. . . yeap, I can see it, you have the 'spirit of rebellion' in your eyes.' And I started bawling, like deep bawling from my soul."

For many, questioning led to profound identity crises:

> "Distrusting established theology was distrust of the God who is mysterious. Anytime the intuition started to say something isn't right, you would smack them down; intuition was treated like a tempting influence rather than a warning influence. The only game in town when you start to doubt is either insanity—divided intention—demonic influence. So, you have a moral deficit, intellectual deficit, spiritual deficit. Those are your only options."

For those who truly wanted to please God, this caused psychological torment:

> "The teaching that you need to trust leaders because they might see something—a blind spot that you can't see. I questioned myself to like insanity because I'm such a deep, introspective person and I want to do the right thing. It's a bit torturous for someone who really wants to please God. It conditioned you, like I lost myself, it really broke me."

Even when preparing to leave, individuals were warned they'd be spiritually punished:

> "Leaving the church would put me at risk for less than God's best. . . I would suffer financially, mentally, and emotionally—everything. I would eventually lose my faith and

turn away from God and end up in Hell, which is eternal conscious torment. It's not a choice anyone would want."

"The Pastor would teach that you had to be strong because you're going to be ridiculed and persecuted. So, you were expecting to be—so if you were questioned by the outside world, of course they are going to tell you that what you believe is not true. It made it very, very, unable to be reached. They make you unable to be reached. It feels like a miracle that I got out. It feels like I ESCAPED something. It was one of the hardest things in my life to leave the church."

The specter of Hell loomed large.

"I was taught that Hell was a real place... very real... the eternal fire. God has rules. His rules are a standard of perfection and if you don't keep on that level—anything that's less than that perfection is sin. If you sin you are destined for eternal Hell unless you get saved—Jesus is the only way."

"There is a requirement to 'live well.' You would be considered not a Christian and when you die you would go to Hell—eternal separation from God."

Perhaps most painfully, participants described the crushing weight of guilt for others' salvation.

"I would literally have days that I was so depressed that like so many people were going to Hell that I really couldn't function... I would have nightmares."

"I felt pressure, because if I don't tell them (those outside the church) about God then they'll be going to Hell and it will be my fault, because they won't be saved. I would feel guilty... a lot of guilt."

These are not abstract concepts—they are *lived realities*.

These are Souls who were simply trying to be "good," trying to belong, trying to love God.

And instead, they were silenced, shamed, and severed from themselves.

THEME TWO:
Cognitive Dissonance

Cognitive dissonance, first coined in 1950 by social psychologist Leon Festinger, describes the deep psychological discomfort that arises when one's actions, beliefs, or values are in conflict. His research with individuals in a doomsday cult revealed that when prophecies failed to come true, many followers did not abandon their beliefs—instead, they became more devoted. The human psyche, Festinger suggested, will often go to great lengths to protect a deeply held belief, even in the face of contradictory evidence.[16]

Social psychologist Elliot Aronson later emphasized that for cognitive dissonance to truly take root, a person must be deeply committed to the belief or behavior in question. As humans, we have a deep need to perceive ourselves as moral, competent, and good. When we feel our actions or questions might violate that identity, dissonance arises[17]—and with it, a soul-deep tension.

Within evangelical communities, where teachings are often presented as *absolute truth* and questioning is seen as rebellion, this internal conflict becomes especially intense. The very desire to be faithful—to be "good before God"—can keep individuals trapped in cycles of silent suffering.

Here is how one participant gave voice to this fear:

> "My biggest fear is that everyone would discount their entire experience with me and say, 'you were lying to us—you must have not been authentic with God' and people will say that I'm not a Christian."

Another participant expressed the heartbreaking experience of trying to reconcile that internal tension:

> "The driver was I wanted to be good. I want to be good before God and this is where God placed me, so I need to figure out how to make this work. You aren't good enough, they don't say that, but you feel it. So, what do I need to do to be good enough. I would question if what I did was right—was I out of line. Being out of line is a message everywhere I go. It makes you wonder what is wrong with you. If you question it you're going to get some form of punishment back."

Again and again, participants described how this dissonance disrupted their ability to trust themselves. Their intuition—the inner compass meant to guide, protect, and help discern—had been replaced by a fear of error, shame, and divine disapproval:

> "The control and lack of freedom and lack of autonomy was the most difficult. Not being able to decide for myself what is good and right."

> "I question why I waited so long... Why didn't I act sooner? What have I not seen? What did I miss? Was I not looking because I didn't see to look or because I didn't want to look?"

> "If you used your intuition to question or had doubts, there was something wrong with you. You're not close enough to God, that's why the doubts are coming—pray more, worship more."

For many, this tension fractured not only their beliefs—but their sense of Self. What began as faithfulness slowly became self-erasure. Their longing to belong and to be "good Christians" forced them to hide their doubts, mask their struggles, and maintain a persona that aligned with what the church expected—even if it meant abandoning their own inner truth.

> "People are not real. You had this façade that you had to maintain about being a 'good' Christian."

"The lack of humanity... the lack of seeing that things are going on and that there are problems. I could see pain in other people, and they would eventually leave because they didn't have space to struggle."

"You live in a constant state of cognitive dissonance—where anytime what I felt was true wasn't aligned with what the church believed—the church always won."

This is the psychological tension that arises when a faith meant to bring peace, connection, and authenticity demands instead that one silence their inner knowing.

This is the wound of dissonance—not simply confusion, but the severing of the Self.

THEME THREE:
Spiritual Bypassing

One of the most insidious forms of spiritual harm within evangelicalism is spiritual bypassing—the act of using religious beliefs or practices to avoid facing emotional pain, unprocessed trauma, or mental health struggles.[18,19] This avoidance is not accidental. It is often deeply embedded in the very fabric of evangelical teachings, where undesirable emotions are repressed, and unquestioning positivity is spiritualized.

The term *spiritual bypassing* was first coined by psychologist John Welwood in 1984 to describe what he called "premature transcendence"—the bypassing of emotional, psychological, or developmental work in an attempt to access spiritual states. Rather than moving through pain toward integration and healing, the bypassing individual skips over it, clinging instead to spiritual ideals that deny the depth of their humanity.[18,19]

In 1987, Dr. Charles Whitfield further expanded on this concept, describing how spiritual bypassing leads people to grasp at the spiritual realm as an escape from the psychological realm—especially from unresolved childhood trauma. His work identified this as a distortion of the healing journey, where individuals attempt to reach spiritual heights while carrying the unacknowledged wounds of their past.[20]

Evangelical theology—with its black-and-white moral structure, its dualistic framing of good versus evil, and its tendency to shame emotional vulnerability—provides the perfect soil for this bypassing to grow. In this environment, spiritual practices become disconnected from emotional truth. Prayer is used to avoid grief. Scripture is weaponized against doubt. And suffering is rebranded as spiritual failure.

The consequences are profound. Shame, emotional numbing, internal confusion, repression, avoidance, fear of anger, toxic positivity, and dissociation are all hallmarks of spiritual bypassing. At its worst, it leads to *spiritual narcissism*—the belief that one's rigid, "correct" theology grants moral superiority over others.[18] The inner voice, the True Self, becomes unreachable. Instead, individuals live with an internalized voice that echoes: *We're right. Everyone else is wrong.*

In my study, participants shared that expressing emotions, especially painful or negative ones, was not allowed in their church communities. These feelings were reinterpreted as spiritual weaknesses or even demonic attacks:

> "There is a lot of satan causing mental illness or anger issues. So, it becomes hard to deal with those problems when you think you just need to rebuke the devil."

> "Any negative emotion or conflict or past thoughts are attributed to 'the enemy is attacking you.' Insecurity is 'of the enemy.' So, I am depressed because I don't trust Jesus—if I trust Jesus more, depression will go away. There is this huge avoidance of not dealing with your problems and not being able to process them with other people. You don't genuinely connect with people. We lack the humanity of each other where everything is spiritual."

Participants consistently reported being discouraged, or outright shamed, from seeking professional help. Mental health was framed as a failure of faith, a sign of insufficient spiritual practice, or evidence of hidden sin:

> "My church had a disdain for secular psychology. If you had a problem it was probably because you weren't following Jesus and satan had a place somewhere—maybe you have sin in your life and you're not dealing with it."

> "I felt that I shouldn't have mental health problems. . . people see you as not holy enough or that you don't have enough faith. You shouldn't be having mental health problems if you are a servant of God—if you are praying and doing all the right things."

Participants were told to rely solely on spiritual practices to manage their mental distress:

> "You had to try harder. At worst they [the church] see therapy as leading you in the wrong direction. At best they see it as a crutch. When what you really ought to do is pray more and read the Bible more. Unpleasant emotions are a spiritual problem—emotions are a false indicator and not to be trusted, PERIOD!"

> "There's no humanity inside the evangelical church. You're either demonized or a sinner if you have a struggle—when you do have a struggle, it's 'pray more,' 'read your Bible more.' It is like 'Oh, can't I have an emotion about something?' There's no room for just being a human. . . there is so much shame around humanity."

Research confirms what these participants shared. Evangelical culture often stigmatizes mental illness, framing it as a result of demons or moral failure. Mental health professionals are viewed with suspicion, and psychiatric medication is often discouraged or denied.[21] Instead, individuals are directed toward pastoral counseling—frequently by those with no training in trauma or psychological care.

The result is tragic. People in need of support are shamed, silenced, and redirected into systems ill-equipped to hold their suffering. Emotions remain unprocessed. Trauma remains unhealed. And the person is left with a spirituality that cannot hold the full truth of who they are.

In bypassing our wounds, we bypass our humanity.

And in bypassing our humanity, *we risk never knowing our Soul.*

THEME FOUR:
Emotional Dissociation / Disconnection from Self

Perhaps one of the most tragic consequences of spiritual abuse is the internal rupture it causes—a severing of a person from their own knowing, their own voice, their own Self.

The teachings within evangelical Christianity often demand that one distrust the Self entirely. You are told that your thoughts are deceptive, your feelings are unreliable, and your desires are sinful. The result is emotional dissociation—a splitting off from one's internal guidance system, a detachment from one's body, emotions, and inner truth.

This messaging generates a profound internal dissonance, a deep weariness that eventually leads to spiritual and emotional disillusionment.[8] You are taught that the very core of who you are is flawed. That something is seriously wrong with you. Over time, this leads to a complete breakdown in self-trust, an erosion of the essential foundation upon which a healthy sense of identity is built.

This disruption goes beyond psychological harm—it interferes with the psychospiritual developmental processes that James Fowler identified as necessary for the formation of a whole, integrated Self. The teaching that "you cannot trust yourself" becomes not just a theological idea, but a lived trauma.

One participant, in the sacred act of reclaiming her voice, expressed:

> "After having these experiences, I was devastated for a season. But now, doing counseling, figuring out my

humanity—letting myself be human and also spiritual at the same time. Out of everything I went through, I learned so much. The one thing that really, truly breaks my heart is how much I listened to a man over God's own voice inside of me."

This grief, *this betrayal of the inner compass*, is echoed by others:

"You are told not to trust yourself—you are supposed to trust God. You are not supposed to trust your own feelings or even your own logic or reasoning. I had to figure out what I believed as my own person. You don't know who the hell you are."

"You were taught that you couldn't trust yourself. I think my lack of confidence comes from not feeling good enough."

"The reason I don't trust myself is because I have lived my entire life in evangelical Christianity. So how many things do I take for granted in my worldview that I'm not even aware of?"

A participant gave voice to the psychological consequences of this split in a powerful and vulnerable reflection:

"OCD was the peak manifestation of me not being able to trust myself. I had to do rituals to seek reassurance and find a pastor who would tell me I was forgiven or whatever in order to feel like I was okay. The most difficult part is being stripped of any kind of control or humanity—and it's turning off of what you know in your gut is true. Literally, there were two sides of me... there was the part of me that totally understood the clinical psychology and what is good for people, and then the part of me that had to flip on my 'Okay, but the real truth is God and this is how we behave here, and this transcends psychology.'"

The cost of this disconnection is not just spiritual, it is existential.

> "There is a part of me missing that I want back, and I don't know how to get it back. I war with it because I really miss God, and now I have kids and I want to guide my children, and I don't know at all what to tell them for my own self. There's a piece of me gone and I want it back."

These words pierce the heart.

When an individual is taught not to trust their own Soul, when their spiritual leaders discourage intuition, suppress emotions, and delegitimize personal experience, the result is deep psychological injury. The messages of shame and unworthiness get embedded into the nervous system and encoded into the psyche.

The teachings of evangelicalism can create traumatic wounds that not only dissociate individuals from themselves but also prevent them from reaching the most sacred stages of faith development: the stages of Unity with the Divine and the Discovery of the True Self.

These are not small wounds. They are sacred injuries—wounds of the Soul.

Wounds that whisper:

> *You are broken.*
> *You are lost.*
> *You cannot be trusted.*

But they are not the end of the story.

These participants, these brave Souls. are walking the long road of healing, reclaiming the voices once silenced, rediscovering the Love that lives within, and remembering who they truly are.

THEME FIVE:
Disenfranchised Grief

Disenfranchised grief, a concept introduced by Dr. Kenneth Doka in the late 1980s, refers to grief that is not acknowledged or validated by society. It is the kind of mourning that lives in the shadows—unseen, unspoken, and unsupported. This form of grief is often complicated, because there is no communal ritual, no space for lament, and no clear language to express the depth of the loss. When unprocessed, it frequently turns inward, leading to self-blame, emotional isolation, or destructive behaviors.[22]

The grief experienced by those who leave abusive religious systems is not often recognized as legitimate. There is no cultural script for mourning the loss of a spiritual identity, the disillusionment of faith, or the betrayal by a community that once claimed to be the embodiment of God's love. And yet, the pain is real. It is immense. And it runs deep.

Participants in this study expressed a profound sense of loss—loss of time, identity, belonging, and spiritual home. One participant shared:

> "It has affected me in a way that's made it harder to create authentic relationships with others. So much of my experience was masking feelings, masking what was really going on because there's no help."

Another participant reflected with quiet sorrow:

> "It makes me sad, there's a whole bunch of wasted time. You look back and your life... WOW... things would have definitely been different."

For those raised within the evangelical system, the grief is especially layered. The teachings were not something they joined—they were the water they swam in, the air they breathed. One participant reflected:

> "I know it has affected me permanently in some ways. I don't see myself ever coming back from that. It's hard because religion harmed me so much. I think if religion was gone the world would be a better place."

> "Being raised in evangelical Christianity—it is woven into who I was all the way back. When you're evangelical for the first 37 years of your life... there's a lot of you that's gonna be till you die. There's so many ways

that I see things that are evangelical that aren't going anywhere. It has left me spiritually homeless."

This grief is not just about losing faith—it is about realizing that what was believed to be love, belonging, and truth, was often control, fear, and illusion. The grief becomes disorienting... because it's not only what you've lost, but the realization that you never truly had what you thought you did. As one participant shared:

> "I'm not grieving the loss of my church home so much now—it's like now what I had was a lie. I am basically grieving that I never had what I thought I had. I have been doing a lot of soul searching, I question everything. It's hard, it's heartbreaking, it's terrifying, and it's devastating."

Others mourned the relational and emotional damage caused by years of indoctrination:

> "There were relationships that could have been much deeper and fuller if I had not come into the relationship with the attitude of I'm going to fix you. I missed out on real authentic, deep relationships. That just makes me sad. I deeply regret that. It is so harmful; it hits you right in your most vulnerable part (places hands directly over her heart). And as I am unpacking spiritual abuse—this is one—this is a really deep type of abuse. It's right in your very being, it's an existential crisis, it's serious stuff."

The emotional toll of this grief is often difficult to express—and even harder to resolve. One Participant gave voice to the deep stuckness that comes from grief without recognition:

> "It's such a trap—it plays on something very healthy in me. Very destructive... I have this background cloud from those experiences... it really is terrible. There is a stuckness in me and a sadness that there's nowhere for me to go to get healthy. I don't know

4 | Spiritual Abuse: Wounding the Immortal Soul

how to get back. I'd like to, I'd like to pray and feel that God is with me. I think I have a pretty deep sadness and something inside me that just... can't move forward, is not free."

And another participant articulated one of the most poignant realities of this grief—that it often goes unseen, unmarked, and unvalidated by society:

"I lost a lot... 13 years of mental health. I lost people, I lost knowledge of myself and my own body. But there's no place to grieve that... there's no tombstone, no cemetery, no ritual that society engages in for that. So, another big impact is this amorphous feeling of grief that I can't explain to anyone."

This is what disenfranchised grief looks like—grief that has no place to land. Grief without a name, a ritual, or a witness.

But here, in these pages, it is being named.

It is being seen.

And that is where healing begins.

PSYCHOSPIRITUAL DAMAGE

The impact of spiritual abuse extends beyond psychological distress—it pierces the very heart of one's being. This form of trauma, rooted in sacred spaces and spiritual authority, causes what can only be described as *psychospiritual damage*.[8] It is not just the mind or body that suffers; it is the Soul that bears the wound.

Participants in this study reported a wide range of symptoms: terror, emotional exhaustion, helplessness, depression, panic attacks, shame, grief, and physical ailments. Many described feeling shattered—disoriented by the collapse of belief systems they once held as sacred. Some lost their faith entirely. Others clung to the remnants of a relationship with God, now fragile and uncertain. For many, what had once been a refuge had become the source of their deepest pain.

And yet, within the grief, a quiet thread of freedom began to emerge.

> "Now it's like. . . it feels good to finally be FREE. It feels more free."

> "I am closer to God now, even though I understand Him way less. I feel free. I felt liberated when I walked away from evangelical Christianity. I am free to ask questions. I am free to make my own decisions without someone calling me a heretic. Leaving the evangelical church has been the best thing I have ever done. There is so much more to God and the Universe than we were led to believe."

> "I felt free for the first time. I know what true freedom can actually mean—you don't have to constantly look over your shoulder."

> "I would say it is more personal now. My faith is more one-on-one. My faith is more one-on-one. It's more me asking questions and having the feeling that God isn't upset with me. I always had this struggle that I'm doing something wrong, that God was upset with me, but, I feel peace now, knowing He isn't upset with me. It is freeing not to believe those things anymore."

This recurring theme of *freedom*—uttered from the lips of those who walked away from the very place that was meant to bring them life—offers a sobering glimpse into the nature of spiritual trauma. When the act of leaving evokes relief, when liberation begins where religious belonging ends, we must pause and ask: *What kind of God was being preached? What kind of gospel was being lived?*

But not all were able to find freedom. Some remain in the silent ache of spiritual exile. This participant shared with haunting clarity:

> "God's face used to be a sun and it smiled on me, now it is dark. I guess it feels like I'm just going to die not a

4 | Spiritual Abuse: Wounding the Immortal Soul

Christian, not connected to God... that's really sad. That shouldn't be what the church should produce, especially for someone who was willing to give their whole life over to it. I think I really believe in God, but I'm scared of Him, but I really miss Him. All these things I've been through, I thought I would sit and rock my babies and pray for them and I have just been silent. I never thought my relationship with God could be touched."

This is the tragedy of spiritual abuse—it distorts the very face of the Divine.

Another participant offered a reflection that speaks not only to the harm, but to the possibility of redemption through love:

"If a religious or spiritual framework is being used by a person—whether they are doing it consciously or not—to mitigate shame or to feel that they are certain because their lives feel very chaotic, I think it most always will be very unhelpful for them and very unhelpful for the people around them. When religion or spirituality is used to give a person an intentional lens so that they can ask themselves in any given interaction 'Is this allowing me to love God and love my neighbor?' then I think it can be something very beautiful and very helpful. And love defined as 'what is experienced as love,' not what weird abstract version of love is being taught by an institutional authority. And if the answer is yes and your religion or spirituality got you there, then I think that's really beautiful and I think that's a big part of what it means to follow Jesus."

This is the essence of psychospiritual recovery: not simply reclaiming a belief system, but rediscovering Love—**real Love**, lived Love, embodied Love.

The participants in this study have endured an invisible trauma—one often denied, minimized, or misunderstood. And yet, their stories ring with the ache of holy longing. They describe not just the trauma of lost beliefs, but the sacred rupture of a stolen intimacy with God and Self.

Their suffering is real. Their grief is deep. And their courage is unmatched.

Many are still in therapy, still unpacking the damage, still wrestling with questions that have no easy answers. Some have found support in online communities or safe friendships; others continue to walk their healing path in quiet solitude. Their coping strategies vary, but nearly all shared one essential truth:

This is real. This has wounded my Soul.

This is not simply psychological trauma, it is an assault on the *immortal self*—the sacred inner life where one's truest essence dwells. And that is why it must be named.

May we never again allow a theology of fear to disguise itself as faith.

May we never again let control be mistaken for care.

May we begin to build spaces where the Soul can breathe again—where questions are welcomed, where **Love** is the measure, and where the Divine is not weaponized, but *whispered*.

••••••

Hearing the experiences of these participants broke my heart. As I transcribed their stories, I wept. Not just from empathy—but from the deep ache of my soul crying out to God with the unbearable weight of what these precious souls, and so many others, have endured. I **knew** this work was Divinely guided. I **knew** it mattered. I **knew** it was time.

This research is for every person who was taught that God is unloving, unreachable, or conditional. For those told they had to earn Love through obedience, perfection, and suppression. That is *not* the God I know. That is not the relationship I have with Jesus. The Divine I experience is a wellspring of unconditional Love—gentle, present, and wholly trustworthy. It is a Love that welcomes you as you are, not as someone else insists you should be.

This work is the culmination of a lifetime of listening—to the whispers of Spirit I felt as a child, and to the sacred task I've carried in my heart ever since. I am standing now, like Todd in *Dead Poets Society*, on the metaphorical desk of my life, raising my voice to say: *O Captain! My Captain!*

I will not be silent.

I will not betray what I know to be True.

This is my moment to resist the structures that have twisted Love into fear, and instead reveal the beauty of a spirituality rooted in freedom, tenderness, and deep trust. It is time to protect the innocent. To stand between them and the teachings that have done such harm. To tell them that they are not broken. That they have never been separate. That the Divine has never left them.

This work is for the souls caught in the crossfire of a faith that could not contain their spiritual growth. For those who, in attempting to progress along the sacred path of faith, were shamed, silenced, or cast out. Evangelicalism, with its rigid doctrines and fear-based control, has created wounds that fracture the very Soul. These wounds sever the connection to the True Self and block the most beautiful stage of psychospiritual development—Union with the Divine.

These souls have endured *ineffable trauma*—a suffering so deep it has no words. But I see them. I honor them. And I offer this work as a pathway toward healing, remembrance, and sacred reclamation.

CHAPTER 4 SUMMARY
Spiritual Abuse: Wounding the Immortal Soul

Spiritual abuse is an esoteric form of trauma—one that devastates not only the mind and body, but the very soul of a person. Among all the forms of psychological and emotional harm, this particular kind strikes at the sacred core of a Being. Within the evangelical Christian community, toxic teachings and dogmatic practices have inflicted deep, enduring wounds on those seeking only to love God, to belong, and to do what is right. One of the most revealing, and heartbreaking, findings in this study was the consistent testimony from participants that *there is no humanity allowed* within this system. Sincere, caring individuals—those earnestly trying to be "good" and faithful—were instead taught that their very humanity was shameful and unworthy. This belief shattered their sense of inner safety, created profound confusion, and ultimately led to a painful disconnection from Self.

This phenomenological study was conducted through interviews with ten participants across the United States. Each had been involved in an evangelical Christian community for at least five years and self-identified as having experienced spiritual abuse. Using Heidegger's hermeneutic phenomenology and a philosophical framework for data analysis, five core themes emerged:

1. Religious Indoctrination
2. Cognitive Dissonance
3. Spiritual Bypassing
4. Emotional Dissociation / Disconnection from Self
5. Disenfranchised Grief

Religious Indoctrination is the psychological conditioning that compels individuals to accept a group's doctrine without question. Under constant pressure and manipulation, individuals unconsciously undergo *resocialization*—replacing their former identity with a new one constructed by the community. This is not free choice; it is a survival response to unbearable spiritual coercion.

Cognitive Dissonance, a term coined by social psychologist Leon Festinger, describes the psychological tension that arises when one's behaviors and beliefs are in conflict. Within the evangelical framework, participants were forced to suppress their doubts, their logic, and their intuition in order to remain aligned with the group. To challenge a belief, no matter how harmful, was to risk eternal consequences. The result was internal fragmentation and a devastating violation of the Self.

Spiritual Bypassing, as described by psychologist John Welwood, occurs when spirituality is used to avoid difficult emotions and unhealed trauma. In the evangelical context, pain is often dismissed as demonic, mental health struggles are labeled as sin, and spiritual teachers are followed without question. These dynamics prevent genuine healing and obstruct the path of spiritual maturity. Spiritual bypassing replaces transformation with toxic positivity and leads to the repression of Self, the loss of inner authority, and spiritual narcissism.

Emotional Dissociation and Disconnection from Self emerged as one of the most painful themes. Evangelical teachings often demanded that individuals distrust their emotions, ignore their inner voice, and relinquish their intuition. This produced a deep and lasting split between the individual and their authentic Self. Participants described losing access to who they truly were, becoming strangers to their own inner life—a disconnection so profound it created spiritual paralysis.

Disenfranchised Grief, a term developed by Dr. Kenneth Doka, refers to grief that is not socially acknowledged or supported. For these participants, there was no communal space to mourn the losses inflicted by spiritual abuse. They grieved lost years, lost relationships, lost identity, and lost trust. Some grieved the God they once loved, now veiled by fear or silence. Without a recognized ritual or language to process their grief, many lived with an aching sorrow that was invisible to those around them.

Ultimately, these teachings and experiences prevented participants from progressing through the natural stages of faith development. As Dr. James Fowler describes, psychospiritual growth requires trust in Self, spiritual individuation, and integration. Evangelicalism, through its harmful doctrines and suppression of inner wisdom, arrested this sacred progression—cutting individuals off from the possibility of Union with the Divine and the Discovery of their Truest Self.

What these participants experienced was not simply religious confusion or disillusionment, it was a *trauma to the Soul*.

Table 4.1 | Participant's experience of sub-themes*

Sub-Themes	P1	P2	P3	P4	P5	P6	P7	P8	P9	P10
Control/Manipulation	•	•	•	•	•	•	•	•	•	•
Pressure to perform	•		•	•	•	•	•	•	•	•
Spiritual Hierarchy	•		•	•	•	•	•	•	•	•
Judgment/Shame/Doubt	•	•	•	•	•	•	•	•	•	•
Mental Health seen as spiritual weakness	•		•	•	•	•	•	•	•	•
Dogmatic teaching	•	•	•	•	•	•	•	•	•	•
No room for humanity	•		•	•	•		•	•	•	•

*Responses from research question one. See Appendix for details.

Table 4.2 | Participant's experience of sub-themes**

Sub-Themes	P1	P2	P3	P4	P5	P6	P7	P8	P9	P10
Lack of humanity No real relationships	•	•	•	•	•	•		•		•
Distrust in religious people	•	•	•		•	•		•	•	•
Lots of therapy	•	•	•	•	•	•				•
Online communities	•	•	•	•	•	•	•	•	•	•
Question everything	•	•	•	•	•	•	•	•	•	•

**Responses from research question three. See Appendix for details.

Part Two Summary

Unveiling the Wound:
How Evangelicalism Harms the Soul

Throughout history, philosophers and theologians alike have spoken of the Soul as the most sacred and eternal aspect of our being. Plato taught that the Soul carries memory from before birth and yearns for liberation. Aristotle saw it as the vital essence that grants us the capacity to grow into our highest potential. Philo believed the Soul was a fragment of the Divine itself—a breath of God animating our humanity. Centuries later, neuroscience has begun to echo these truths. Dr. Antonio Damasio asserts that the mind and body are not separate—that the Soul is the indivisible essence of our conscious being. Neuroimaging studies reveal that religious and spiritual experiences register in the brain as deep emotional responses rooted in trust, suggesting that the longing for the Divine is not only spiritual, but biological.

Dr. Lisa Miller's research takes this even further, showing us that the brain is innately wired for connection with something greater. She describes this capacity as the "awakened brain"—a neural circuitry designed to perceive spiritual truths and experience inner peace, healing, and wholeness. What emerges from these perspectives is a shared recognition that the Soul is not a metaphor, *it is the very heart of who we are.* And when this Soul is harmed, particularly through spiritual abuse, the consequences are devastating.

Spiritual abuse is not simply emotional manipulation or religious overreach—it is a deep violation of the immortal Self. It distorts one's image of God, severs trust in the inner voice, and poisons the sacred terrain of the heart. Those who experience it are often taught that they are inherently evil, that their worth is conditional, and that Love must be earned through perfection and performance. They are told not to trust themselves, not to feel, not to question. As a result, many find themselves locked in an endless pursuit of belonging—afraid that any misstep could cast them out of the grace they've been taught is fragile and fleeting.

This form of abuse is uniquely cruel because it targets the place within us where we experience Love, meaning, and Divine connection. It replaces wonder with fear, intimacy with obligation, and sacred mystery with rigid control. It is a betrayal that goes unseen by most of society, leaving its survivors disoriented, grief-stricken, and spiritually exiled.

Evangelicalism, when steeped in rigid dogma, often functions as a subculture fueled by control, exclusivity, and moral absolutism. Its teachings, when weaponized, create traumatic wounds that fragment the psyche and disconnect individuals from their internal compass. In this system, suffering is spiritualized, silence is sanctified, and questioning is demonized. Dissociation becomes a survival mechanism—an invisible splitting of self that leaves unresolved trauma buried deep in the Soul.

Spiritual abuse creates what can only be described as psychospiritual damage. It is trauma directed not just at the mind or emotions, but at the sacred core of a person. It disrupts the developmental unfolding of faith, silencing the soul's natural progression toward individuation, freedom, and intimacy with the Divine. It prevents the journey toward union—toward the final, radiant stages of faith described by Fowler, where one transcends ego and encounters the Mystery of God in wholeness and Love.

To those who have lived through this, your story matters. Your healing matters. The road back to your True Self may feel long, but it is possible. The Love you were taught to fear is still within you, still holding you, still calling you Home.

> You are not lost.
> You are not alone.
> *You are a Soul—Deeply and Eternally Loved.*

PART THREE

The Inner Architecture
of Understanding:
A Sacred Invitation to the Research

Part Three

This section offers a deeper look into the heart of this work: the findings of my research and the theoretical framework that guided this study. While preparing this manuscript, I wrestled with whether to include this chapter. Would it feel too academic? Too formal? Would it disrupt the flow of the lived experiences and truths already shared?

In the end, I chose to include it—because I believe it matters. Not just to scholars or clinicians, but to anyone seeking to understand spiritual abuse with the reverence and clarity it deserves.

This part of the journey speaks to the science, the structure, and the philosophical roots of this esoteric form of trauma. It may feel more methodical in form, but beneath every paragraph lives a heartbeat of deep care and purpose. The research methodology described here provided the container to hold the voices of those who were brave enough to share their pain. It gave structure to their stories, language to their longings, and grounding to a phenomenon that too often remains unseen.

So, to you, the reader, *thank you.*

> Thank you for arriving here with curiosity and care.
>
> Thank you for wanting to learn more—not just with your mind, but with your heart.
>
> Thank you for your willingness to expand your understanding and question long-held assumptions.
>
> Thank you for being part of the healing movement.

This is how change begins:

> Not through force, but through *awareness*.
>
> Not through certainty, but through *compassion*.
>
> Not by rushing past the pain, but by *turning gently toward it*.

What follows is a framework—a sacred map—for how we can begin to understand the deep psychological, emotional, and spiritual impact of spiritual abuse. It is both rigorous and tender. May it serve you well on your journey.

5

Damaging Doctrines

"Once I began to realize that there were no rules and that my path didn't have to look like everyone else's, I relaxed and my whole world opened up."

—G. BRIAN BENSON

The purpose of this qualitative phenomenological study was to explore the impact of spiritual abuse within the evangelical Christian community in the United States. With reverence for both science and soul, this chapter unveils what emerged from the stories entrusted to this research—stories filled with heartbreak, courage, confusion, and transformation.

This study was designed to illuminate the lived experiences of those who encountered spiritual abuse within evangelicalism, to examine the implications this form of trauma has on one's connection to self, and to deepen the collective understanding of spiritual abuse by integrating scholarly literature with the sacred voices of those affected. In doing so, this research contributes a vital perspective to the counseling profession and the wider psychological community—one that calls for trauma-informed care that is also spiritually sensitive and culturally attuned.

To frame this inquiry, I utilized an integrative theoretical lens that views religion not only as a belief system, but as a profound meaning-making structure, an attachment bond, and a moral compass. The theoretical framework draws from multiple disciplines within psychology to understand the full weight of spiritual abuse on the human soul.

Attribution Theory, as originally developed by Weiner and later applied to religion by Spilka, guided the exploration of how individuals make sense of their experiences—especially in the context of suffering. Attributions are the internal stories we tell about why things happen. These frameworks include dimensions of locus of control (whether the cause lies within or outside the self), stability (whether the cause is temporary or permanent),[1,2,3,4,5] and controllability (whether one has any power over the event). Within a spiritual context, these attributions often take on profound significance: "Is this happening because I displeased God?" "Is this suffering part of a test?" "What did I do wrong?" The very framing of these questions reveals the psychospiritual terrain being navigated.

Spilka's religious attribution theory adds further depth, suggesting that religion is often used to explain life's most painful and confusing events. It influences three psychological goals: the need to understand, the need to feel control, and the need to protect one's self-worth. When spiritual teachings distort these goals, through shame, fear, or authoritarian control, the individual's entire worldview can collapse—resulting in deep psychological fragmentation.[6]

Attachment Theory, as adapted by Granqvist for spiritual contexts, also informed this study. Divine Attachment theory examines how early relational patterns are often projected onto the Divine. For many, God becomes a parental figure—a protector, nurturer, or, tragically, a punishing authority. When spiritual abuse occurs within this framework, it doesn't merely break trust in people, it shatters trust in the very nature of love, safety, and belonging.[7]

Religious Coping Theory, as developed by Kenneth Pargament, provided another critical layer of understanding. Spiritual abuse distorts one's religious orienting system—the internal compass that helps one make sense of life, cope with suffering, and connect with the sacred. When religion becomes a source of trauma instead of healing, that compass spins wildly, leaving the person unanchored, disoriented, and disconnected from what once brought them peace.[8]

Through these layered lenses, the findings of this study reveal not only the recurring themes of spiritual abuse within the evangelical church, but also the profound effects on self-trust, emotional regulation, identity development, and spiritual wellbeing. What emerged from the voices of the participants was more than data—it was a call to see, to listen, and to respond with wisdom and compassion.

This chapter will walk through those findings—each one a reflection of the inner world of those who dared to speak their truth.

May their courage open our hearts.

May their insights illuminate a better way forward.

DISCUSSION OF FINDINGS

The profound impact that trauma has on every dimension of a person's life—mind, body, and spirit—has been widely studied over the past few decades. Research in neuroscience, psychology, education, religion, and the health sciences has expanded our understanding of trauma's long-term effects on neurodevelopment, emotional regulation, and interpersonal functioning. Yet, one dimension remains vastly underexplored: the trauma of spiritual abuse, and its devastating effect on the formation and integration of the Self.

This gap is particularly striking when we recognize how deeply intertwined spiritual experience is with identity development. While other forms of trauma are increasingly met with therapeutic understanding and support, spiritual abuse, especially within systems that claim to nurture the soul, remains largely invisible. This study set out to change that.

There are three pivotal windows in neurodevelopment: the final trimester of pregnancy, the first three years of life, and adolescence. During these formative stages, the brain encodes perception, emotion, and belief at an implicit level—creating automatic responses that shape how one relates to the world and to oneself. Unless disrupted by significant insight or transformative experience, these deeply ingrained beliefs become the foundation of a person's reality.[9]

For many participants in this study, the disruption came in the form of what has been called the Deconstruction of Faith—a process where long-held spiritual beliefs are questioned, unraveled, and often dismantled. It is a painful reckoning, but also an invitation to growth.

Spiritual abuse, particularly within the evangelical Christian church, was reported by participants as interfering with the foundational neurodevelopmental process of *becoming oneself*. They shared that for years, even decades, they lived in a state of spiritual performance, emotional suppression, and existential disconnection. Many expressed that only after leaving the evangelical system did they begin the process of asking: *Who am I, really?*

One of the most haunting insights that emerged from this research was a shared sentiment among participants: that their *humanity was not allowed* in the environments they were part of. Their vulnerability, questions, doubts, desires, and emotional needs were not welcome. These core parts of being human were seen as weak, sinful, or dangerous.

This type of suppression has far-reaching consequences. The *development of the Self*, as supported in the literature, is deeply rooted in our spiritual experiences and social interactions. The final stage of Self-construction is often referred to as the emergence of the *Spiritual Self*—a space where individuals find meaning, resilience, connection, and personal transformation. But for those trapped within rigid and authoritarian belief systems, the pathway to this sacred emergence is obstructed.

According to Janoff-Bulman's Theory of Shattered Assumptions, three beliefs are central to a person's psychological well-being:[10,11]

1. The world is benevolent, and people are generally good.
2. Life is meaningful, and good things happen to good people.
3. The self is worthy, and has some measure of control over life's outcomes.

The findings from this study reveal that *evangelical doctrine actively dismantles all three*. Participants were taught that humans are inherently depraved, that the world is corrupt and must be escaped, and that they are powerless and unworthy without divine intervention. These teachings shattered participants' sense of self, security, and meaning—leaving deep psychological and spiritual wounds in their place.

And yet, growth often begins in the rupture.

Consistent with existing psychological theories of development and spiritual change, the breakdown of these toxic constructs can serve as the *gateway to individuation, spiritual maturity*, and *faith reconstruction*. The participants in this study were each undergoing this very process. Through grief, confusion, and courage, they were beginning to reclaim their spiritual agency. They were learning how to hold their questions without fear, and to rediscover their connection to the Divine in a way that felt intimate, authentic, and free.

But this process has not been easy. Many described the experience of *spiritual homelessness*—a term that reflects not only the loss of a community, but the rupture in their very understanding of God and self. What should have been a supported transition into a deeper stage of faith development was instead met with condemnation, ostracism, and spiritual abandonment.

This is not how it's meant to be.

In Fowler's Stages of Faith Development, questioning and wrestling with beliefs is not a departure from faith, it is an advancement of it. The transition from Stage Three: Synthetic-Conventional Faith to Stage Four: Individuative-Reflective Faith is a sacred passage into maturity.[12] Yet evangelical systems, by design, resist this passage. They silence the seekers, punish the questioners, and exile the ones who begin to wake up. As a result, people become stuck—arrested in their development and unable to move toward the freedom, intimacy, and union that characterizes the highest stages of spiritual growth.

The participants in this study are among the brave ones. Their voices reveal not only the pain of spiritual abuse but the resilience of the human spirit. They are truth-seekers. Soul survivors. Each of them is walking the narrow path of reconstructing their lives and rediscovering their connection to Love—on their own terms, in their own way.

This research reveals a profound truth: *spiritual abuse is not merely doctrinal or behavioral, it is existential.* It impacts one's view of self, others, the Divine, and the very nature of reality. It is trauma that strikes at the Soul.

And yet, even in the shadows of this pain, healing is possible. The path is not linear. It is a spiral of remembering, releasing, and returning—to the body, to the heart, and ultimately, to the Sacred center within.

DOCTRINAL HARM AND PSYCHOLOGICAL IMPACT

The scientific literature reviewed for this study identified several core doctrines within the evangelical Christian church that were found to be profoundly damaging to the human psyche and the development of the Self. This phenomenological research not only affirms those scholarly findings but also brings them to life through the lived experiences of real people—Souls who have carried the invisible wounds of spiritual abuse for much of their lives. The voices of the participants confirm, with raw vulnerability, the deeply traumatic effects these teachings can have.

Eternal Damnation

All ten participants were familiar with the doctrine of eternal conscious torment—a literal hell, where the unredeemed are forever separated from God in agony. Many spoke of being utterly terrified as children, internalizing the belief that one misstep, one wrong thought, could doom them to eternity in that place. One participant even traced the development of Obsessive-Compulsive Disorder (OCD) to this terror. These findings are consistent with Dr. Marlene Winell's research, which concluded that religious teachings centered on fear of divine punishment can lead to chronic anxiety and perfectionism. The fear of hell, embedded from childhood, left participants in a state of unrelenting dread, afraid not only of failure, but of being beyond forgiveness.

Conversion and Salvation

Closely tied to the fear of damnation is the evangelical requirement of a conversion experience—an internalized "moment" of being saved, typically through a prescribed prayer or act of repentance. Participants described this as the "magic prayer," and many shared that they prayed it hundreds of times, hoping it would "stick." Instead of providing comfort, this doctrine created intense anxiety and spiritual confusion. They were left unsure if they were ever truly saved, and as a result, constantly questioned their worthiness, salvation, and standing with God. Even among participants who no longer believe in a literal hell, the psychological residue of this fear lingers. The uncertainty around their salvation led to chronic guilt, self-doubt, and paralyzing indecisiveness—an internal war between indoctrination and intuition.

Evangelism and the Weight of Responsibility

Another source of spiritual trauma was the obligation to evangelize—to share the gospel with others in order to "save" them from eternal punishment. Several participants recalled having nightmares as children, terrified that friends, family members, or classmates would go to hell because they hadn't shared the message of salvation. For a child to carry that kind of weight is emotionally crushing. Participants expressed deep sorrow over the loss of real connection with others, admitting that they had been taught to view people not as whole beings to love, but as souls to rescue. One participant wept over missed opportunities for deep friendship, reflecting on how the focus on conversion robbed them of authentic human connection.

Original Sin and the Inherent Evil of the Self

Perhaps the most soul-wounding doctrine reported was that of original sin—the belief that each person is born inherently sinful, broken, and separate from God. Participants echoed this repeatedly: they were taught they were evil from birth, incapable of trusting their own thoughts, desires, or emotions. They were not to rely on themselves but only on Scripture, pastors, and external authority. This doctrine interrupts the natural process of individuation—the healthy psychological development of self-trust and autonomy. Participants described this as a trap, a prison of the mind and soul. They reported years of shame, indecisiveness, and learned helplessness. They had been conditioned to believe they were flawed beyond repair, and without access to their inner guidance or agency, many struggled to make even basic life decisions. This is consistent with Winell's findings, which liken this state to a double-bind—a psychological setup in which one is told they are responsible for their own redemption, yet simultaneously incapable of achieving it on their own.

Dispensationalist Eschatology and the Rapture

One of the most emotionally destabilizing doctrines discussed was dispensationalist eschatology—the belief in a future "rapture" when the righteous will be taken to Heaven, and everyone else will be left behind to endure tribulation. Nearly all participants reported traumatic childhood memories associated with this teaching. Some shared that they would wake up from nightmares, run to their parents' room to see if they were still there—desperate to ensure they hadn't been left behind. This is not a metaphor. This is trauma. These teachings sow seeds of existential terror, leading to chronic spiritual hypervigilance. They also propagate spiritual bypassing—the idea that negative emotions are distractions from faith or signs of weakness. In this framework, suffering is not to be felt or explored; it is to be transcended. Participants internalized the message that their pain must be denied, their doubts suppressed, and their full emotional life kept hidden. The result?

Profound disconnection from the Self and an inability to integrate one's own suffering into a healthy, embodied spirituality.

Authority and the Psychological Trap of Obedience

Perhaps one of the most insidious and damaging doctrines identified by participants was the elevation of religious leaders as unquestionable spiritual authorities—individuals placed by God, whose teachings were to be followed without resistance. Participants described a culture in which to question leadership was to question God Himself. This created an intense psychological trap: you must suppress your intuition, silence your voice, and conform in order to remain accepted, blessed, and spiritually safe. Several participants described this system as one where "thinking for yourself" was seen as rebellion. They were conditioned to see submission as virtue and autonomy as sin.

The result of this hierarchical, authoritarian structure is a *repression of the basic human need for inquiry, autonomy, and spiritual discernment*. Participants described being shamed, silenced, and emotionally isolated for bringing forward even the gentlest questions. The cost of honesty was spiritual exile. The cost of doubt was condemnation.

MENTAL HEALTH, STIGMATIZATION, AND THE SILENT SUFFERING OF THE SOUL

Among the most disturbing findings from both this study and the supporting literature is the way mental health is viewed within the evangelical Christian church. Across denominations, mental illness is routinely spiritualized—dismissed not as a legitimate health concern, but as a symptom of weak faith, personal sin, or even demonic influence. One study cited in the literature revealed that over 41% of individuals with mental health needs reported their symptoms were ignored, minimized, or outright rejected by their evangelical church communities. These individuals were often discouraged, or even forbidden, from seeking professional help from trained psychologists or mental health providers.[13] This staggering statistic was echoed even more strongly in this study: 100% of participants confirmed that mental health issues in their evangelical communities were viewed as spiritual failings.

Again and again, participants reported that their mental health struggles were met not with compassion or clinical guidance, but with well-meaning yet deeply harmful responses: "pray harder," "read your Bible more," "rebuke the enemy." Instead of receiving care, they were handed spiritual platitudes and doctrinal reprimands. Left untreated and misunderstood, their emotional suffering deepened.

Some lived with undiagnosed anxiety or depression for decades. Some suffered silently with trauma-related disorders. Many described how the pressure to suppress or spiritualize their suffering compounded their pain, creating cycles of shame, isolation, and self-blame. What they needed was presence, empathy, and healing support. What they received was silence, dismissal, and spiritual condemnation.

The psychological impact of these teachings, compounded over time, was devastating. Participants in this study articulated symptoms aligned with psychospiritual trauma: terror, helplessness, hopelessness, depression, dissociation, anxiety, profound shame, guilt, and a paralyzing sense of spiritual and emotional loss. Many expressed anger and grief so deep it touched the core of their being. For some, their experience within evangelicalism led to a complete collapse of faith—not because they no longer sought the Divine, but because the version of God they had been taught was incompatible with Love.

One participant shared, "I lost part of myself, and I want it back." She had only been part of an evangelical community from the age of 14 to 22. Yet, now in her early 40s, she still carries the ache of that soul wound. Hers is not an isolated story. Every participant in this study bore witness to the lasting emotional and spiritual injuries inflicted during their time within these communities.

Perhaps most sobering is the realization that millions of individuals and children across the United States may be enduring this kind of trauma right now—unseen, unheard, and unacknowledged.

Their suffering is hidden behind Sunday smiles and silenced beneath the weight of doctrines that deny their humanity. They are told they are broken because they are anxious. They are told they lack faith because they are depressed. They are told they are selfish for seeking boundaries, help, or truth.

And if they dare to challenge these teachings, if they dare to ask questions or voice their pain—they risk being labeled rebellious, deceived, or even demonic. They are pushed to disconnect from their bodies, their emotions, their inner knowing. As Hoffman's research confirmed, this creates an unbearable psychological double-bind. They bury their truth beneath a constructed spiritual persona—a *false self*—built for acceptance, not wholeness. To survive, they dissociate. They fragment.

This is existential trauma. It cuts to the root of who we are. And for many, the result is a profound disconnection from their inner life, their relationships, their identity, and their sense of the Divine.

The findings of this study reveal that the damage done within this theological system does not merely affect behavior or belief—it alters *the very architecture of the Soul*. The deep spiritual injuries described here are not abstract or exaggerated. They are real. They are enduring. And they are *preventable*.

It is time to acknowledge the pain. To name the harm. And to create safe spaces where the Immortal Self can be seen, held, and slowly remembered.

UNDERSTANDING THE INNER LANDSCAPE OF SPIRITUAL ABUSE

General Attribution Theory: The Soul's Search for Meaning

At the heart of spiritual experience is a deeply human longing to understand our place in the world—to know *why* we are here, what we are meant to do, and how we are held by the Divine in the face of suffering. General Attribution Theory offers a profound lens through which to understand how individuals make sense of life's events, especially within religious frameworks. It proposes that causal attributions—the beliefs we form about the origins of our experiences—are essential to how we navigate meaning, control, and identity.[1]

Religious systems, particularly those embedded within evangelical Christianity, offer structured explanations for creation, suffering, salvation, and human destiny. They prescribe rituals, define moral codes, and provide frameworks that help people assign meaning to both blessings and adversities. But what happens when these meaning-making structures themselves become a source of harm?

For every participant in this study, spiritual abuse dismantled their previously held attributions. Their beliefs about God, sin, salvation, prayer, and personal worth—once accepted as sacred truth—were destabilized. Their meaning systems were disrupted, their sense of personal agency challenged, and their self-worth deeply altered.

Many shared that their drive to remain in these environments was rooted in love, devotion, and a sincere desire to "be a good Christian," "do the right thing," or "please God." These attributions had once provided a sense of safety and spiritual orientation, but as their lived experiences began to contradict these beliefs, they were forced into a courageous reckoning. That disruption, though painful, was also the spark that allowed them to examine their beliefs and begin to reclaim personal agency and redefine the nature of Love, Faith, and Self.

Weiner's Attribution Theory:
Powerlessness, Punishment, and the Erosion of Trust

To further understand the psychological toll of spiritual abuse, this study applied Weiner's Attribution Theory, which explores three critical dimensions: locus of control, stability, and controllability. Each of these reveals how belief systems either empower or disempower the individual—how they shape one's view of responsibility, hope, and personal value.[2]

Locus of Control

In evangelical systems, the locus of control is almost always external. Pastors, leaders, and church authorities are perceived as holding spiritual authority ordained by God—leaving the individual dependent, deferential, and often silenced. Every participant in this study shared that they were taught not to trust themselves. To question the leader was to question God. This externalization of authority undermined their self-trust and, over time, deeply eroded their sense of identity and personal worth.

Stability

The dimension of stability reflects whether the cause of an outcome is seen as fixed or changeable. Within evangelicalism, the system is experienced as unchangeable—a stable, unyielding structure where deviation from its rigid rules results in guilt, shame, and exclusion. When participants felt unable to meet its expectations, they did not experience correction or compassion, they experienced despair. Over time, this creates what psychology calls *learned helplessness*— a loss of hope that things can be different. Many participants shared feeling trapped in a system that would never change, and from which there seemed no escape.

Controllability

The final dimension, controllability, explores whether outcomes are perceived as the result of personal effort or external forces. In evangelical teachings, "sin" is viewed as a moral failure—completely within the individual's control. This belief leads to harsh judgment and punitive responses toward those within the community who struggle. Ironically, those outside the church, the "unsaved," are often treated with more compassion because they are viewed as lost rather than willfully disobedient.

This creates a disturbing paradox: those who are most deeply committed to the faith are often met with the least grace. As one participant insightfully expressed, the moment you are "saved," you stop being seen with compassion and start being measured by your performance. Any perceived failure is not met with empathy, but with condemnation.

The Spiritual Cost of Attributional Harm

These attributional patterns—of control, helplessness, and blame—deeply distort the individual's inner world. They create psychological traps, where suffering is met not with support but with spiritualized blame. They disrupt the development of autonomy, empathy, and resilience. And most tragically, they fracture one's ability to experience a loving connection with God and with one's own Soul.

This study's findings reveal that spiritual abuse does not merely create emotional distress. It reprograms the very way people interpret reality. It distorts their understanding of suffering, responsibility, and belonging. It convinces them they are broken—and that God agrees.

But as these participants bravely began to examine their beliefs, question their inherited attributions, and listen once more to their own intuition, they began to uncover a truth far more liberating:

They were never broken. They were never unworthy. And they have always been free to return to the Love that was never lost.

Granqvist's Divine Attachment Theory: Healing Our Sacred Bond

One of the most profound insights into the psychology of spirituality comes from Granqvist's Divine Attachment Theory, which explores how we relate to the Divine as an attachment figure—just as we might to a parent, partner, or caregiver. This theory suggests that our relationship with God is not just theological or doctrinal, it is *relational*. It carries the emotional imprints of security or insecurity, intimacy or fear, comfort or distance.[7]

In the evangelical Christian context, many participants in this study internalized an image of God that was rigid, angry, demanding, or emotionally unavailable. Over time, this produced what Granqvist describes as *insecure attachment*—a spiritual relationship marked by anxiety, shame, and a deep fear of rejection or punishment. When one's attachment to God is insecure, it often results in psychological distress: depression, anxiety, self-doubt, and emotional disconnection.[14],[15]

But something extraordinary happened when these participants began to deconstruct their inherited faith and leave these environments behind. Outside of the confines of the evangelical system, many shared that they began to encounter the Divine in new, unexpected, and healing ways. One participant expressed, "I can finally know who God is." Another described God not as a wrathful judge but as a "*Maternal Nurturer*"—a presence of gentleness, comfort, and peace. For many, their faith didn't end when they left the church, it began.

Granqvist's theory affirms what these participants discovered: that a *secure* attachment to the Divine leads to greater tolerance, openness to exploration, emotional resilience, and a deeper sense of connection to self and others. When God is experienced as a safe haven and secure base, spirituality becomes not a source of fear, but a source of rest.[16]

What we believe about God shapes how we see ourselves. If God is distant, we may feel we are unworthy of closeness. If God is angry, we may feel perpetually at fault. But if God is Love—as many participants came to rediscover—then we begin to realize that we, too, are worthy of love, belonging, and spiritual freedom. As one participant put it, "God isn't upset with me anymore. He never was."

What we believe about the Divine is not just a matter of theology. It is a reflection of our Soul's capacity for intimacy, trust, and healing. And when we are free to reimagine that relationship, we reclaim our right to experience God not as fear, but as Love.

Pargament's Religious Coping Theory: When the Sacred Becomes Unsafe

Religious Coping Theory, developed by Kenneth Pargament, offers another essential framework for understanding how individuals use their faith to navigate suffering and adversity. According to Pargament, religion and spirituality serve as powerful pathways for discovering meaning, gaining a sense of control, feeling comforted, deepening community, and transforming one's life.[8] These coping strategies can be life-giving—or, in some cases, profoundly harmful.

Pargament distinguishes between *positive* and *negative* religious coping. Positive coping involves viewing God as a partner in suffering, feeling supported by the Divine, and believing that spiritual challenges can lead to growth. Negative coping, by contrast, occurs when individuals believe God is punishing, absent, or disappointed in them. It creates isolation instead of comfort, anxiety instead of peace.[17]

The participants in this study offered a sobering insight: in the evangelical system, the Sacred was often not a source of solace, it was a source of torment.

Many participants reported that when they sought help, asked hard questions, or voiced doubt, they were met not with compassion but with condemnation. Their deepest spiritual questions—ones that could have led to growth, healing, and deeper trust—were instead framed as rebellion or spiritual weakness. This created a kind of spiritual crisis: a rupture in their connection with the Divine.

According to Pargament's theory, such ruptures constitute a disruption in the "religious orienting system"—the internal compass that helps us make sense of life in sacred terms. When this compass is manipulated or violated, the result is not only spiritual confusion but deep psychospiritual pain.[17]

Participants shared that their most intimate relationship, their connection with God, was hijacked by fear, control, and conditional acceptance. They were taught that Divine love had to be earned through performance. That God's approval could be lost. That suffering was the result of sin. These beliefs did not offer healing. They inflicted trauma.

Yet, as many participants also expressed, once they left these systems and began to redefine their spirituality, a slow and sacred transformation began. They discovered that God had never abandoned them. That Love had never been earned—it had simply *always been*.

RECLAIMING THE SACRED

These theoretical frameworks reveal what this research has made so deeply clear: spiritual abuse doesn't just hurt feelings—it disorients the very foundations of meaning, identity, and trust. It attacks the core of what it means to be human, to feel loved, and to belong in the Universe.

But the healing begins the moment we question. The moment we wonder if there might be another way to know God. The moment we realize that our pain is not rebellion—it is our Soul crying out for Truth, for Freedom, for Love.

And when we listen to that cry, we begin to return... to ourselves, to our Sacred essence, and to the God who was never the one wounding us in the first place.

THE IMPACT OF THE EVANGELICAL CONVERSION EXPERIENCE

James Fowler's theory of faith development offers a powerful lens for understanding the complexity and potential disruption that can arise from evangelical conversion experiences—particularly those described as being "born again." While such experiences are often celebrated within evangelical subculture as moments of salvation and identity renewal, Fowler issues a clear and compelling caution: when conversion is used as a mechanism to *bury* the pre-conversion self—rather than to revisit, rework, and integrate it—the result can be spiritual stagnation and the formation of what he called an *internal saboteur*.[18]

Fowler emphasizes that authentic conversion is not about bypassing pain or discarding one's past. Instead, it is a *re-centering*—a profound reorientation of value, meaning, and belonging that occurs through a conscious process of internal transformation. It involves the adoption of a new narrative and community, yes, but it must also involve the *recomposing* of earlier stages of self. Without this sacred return to what has been—without the healing recapitulation of the stories, wounds, and truths of the past—conversion remains incomplete.

In the evangelical system, however, participants in this study often encountered a theology that insisted on the *negation* of their former selves. They were told that to be "made new" in Christ meant leaving behind their pain, questioning, and humanity. But when past experiences are denied instead of integrated, the self cannot progress. Psychospiritual development halts. The Soul remains tethered to an earlier stage of faith, unable to move forward into the wholeness it longs for.

Fowler warned that this is especially damaging when it happens to children. A child between the ages of seven and ten who undergoes a premature conversion experience, particularly in a fundamentalist environment, may form what he calls a *precocious identity*. This child takes on adult patterns of belief and religious language before their psyche is developmentally ready to hold them. As a result, the adolescent identity crisis—so essential for individuation and growth, is bypassed—cementing early-stage beliefs as immovable truths. Unless a major life disruption occurs later in adulthood, the child-turned-adult will often remain locked in that early stage of faith for the rest of their life.[18]

This process was reflected in many participants of this study. Those raised within the evangelical subculture described the shaping of their worldview as something that would *"always be with me in some way."* Their stories revealed how deeply ingrained these formative teachings were—especially those regarding original sin, eternal damnation, and submission to spiritual authority. These doctrines weren't simply theological—they became the architecture of identity, worldview, and self-worth.

Children raised in such rigid systems often developed what Winnicott described as a *false self*—a persona constructed to meet the expectations of their community, while their true self remained hidden or exiled.[19] The demands to perform, conform, and please others emotionally—especially God and parental figures—resulted in emotional intimidation, spiritual confusion, and the suppression of individuality.

Trauma at this neurodevelopmental stage has grave consequences. Research shows that trauma during early life can shut down the thalamus—the brain's relay station for sensory information—creating a dissociative response that helps the child survive an environment they cannot escape.[9] For children in abusive religious systems, this dissociation becomes a spiritual strategy: to disconnect from their own thoughts, feelings, and instincts in the name of obedience, holiness, or worthiness.

And yet, this form of trauma—*spiritual trauma*—remains largely unaddressed in both psychological literature and therapeutic practice.

With the rise of the Deconstruction of Faith movement, millions of individuals are re-examining the religious frameworks they once held as absolute. As these people begin to face the fear-based doctrines and psychological entanglements that shaped their understanding of God and self, a new frontier of trauma care is emerging—one that requires deep sensitivity, spiritual humility, and an integrated understanding of faith and psychology.

This qualitative study stands at the threshold of that frontier. It offers a window into the lived experiences of those who have suffered spiritual abuse within the evangelical Christian Church. It begins to name what has long gone unnamed. It illuminates what has remained hidden. It validates what has so often been dismissed or denied.

And perhaps most importantly, it reveals that what was harmed can be healed.

When the Soul is given space to speak its truth, it will always move toward restoration. When the story of the past is revisited with compassion, it can finally be rewritten. When the Self is honored—fully, tenderly, unapologetically—the path toward spiritual wholeness becomes not only possible, but sacred.

CHAPTER 5 SUMMARY
Damaging Doctrines

This qualitative phenomenological study, grounded in multiple theoretical frameworks, illuminated the profound psychological and spiritual impact of spiritual abuse within the evangelical Christian Church. By drawing from frameworks such as General Attribution Theory, Weiner's Attribution Theory, Granqvist's Divine Attachment Theory, Pargament's Religious Coping Theory, and Fowler's Stages of Faith Development, the research offers a multidimensional lens through which to understand this complex and deeply wounding form of trauma.

Through the lens of General Attribution Theory, it became clear that participants experienced a destabilization of their core meaning-making systems. The religious structures they had trusted to provide purpose, moral clarity, and connection instead undermined their autonomy and sense of worth. What once shaped their values and identity became a source of spiritual confusion and psychological harm. Participants courageously questioned the doctrines they were raised with—particularly those centered around performance, worthiness, and salvation—which initiated a journey of reevaluation and inner reclamation.

Weiner's Attribution Theory brought attention to the way evangelical teachings promoted an external locus of control, fostering dependence on hierarchical authority and minimizing the individual's inner voice. Stability within this system was not life-giving but imprisoning—rigid structures that engendered hopelessness and helplessness. Controllability became a mechanism for judgment: "saved" individuals were expected to adhere perfectly to moral standards and punished when they failed, while "unsaved" individuals were met with sympathy and efforts at conversion. This inversion of compassion contributed to profound emotional confusion, fear, and internalized shame.

Granqvist's Divine Attachment Theory helped reveal how participants' attachments to the Divine were often formed through fear, guilt, and conditional acceptance. God was perceived as distant, punitive, and emotionally unreliable. Within the evangelical system, this insecure attachment contributed to psychological distress such as anxiety, spiritual scrupulosity, and depression. Yet strikingly, once outside the system, many participants began to encounter a profoundly different experience of God—one marked by gentleness, peace, and loving presence. For some, this connection blossomed for the first time. A secure attachment to the Divine became a pathway to healing, greater emotional integration, and spiritual freedom.

Informed by Pargament's Religious Coping Theory, the study examined how spiritual abuse distorted participants' ability to engage in positive religious coping. Instead of feeling partnered by the Divine in their suffering, participants often felt abandoned or punished by a harsh and unrelenting God. Their ability to find comfort, meaning, or connection was severely compromised. Spiritual struggle became a defining feature of their experience—one that disrupted their internal compass and fractured their sense of safety within both community and self. The result was psychospiritual distress and wounds inflicted at the deepest levels of meaning, identity, and sacred belonging.

Finally, applying Fowler's Faith Development Theory exposed the spiritual arrest caused by evangelical conversion frameworks. Fowler warns that "born again" experiences, when used to negate the past rather than re-integrate it, interrupt authentic faith development. Rigid teachings, particularly those emphasizing original sin, eternal damnation, and hierarchical submission, stunted the natural unfolding of spiritual maturity and individuation. Children and adults alike were shaped into "false selves," rewarded for suppressing emotion, intuition, and uniqueness in exchange for conformity and acceptance. The long-term impact was existential disorientation and, for many, a sense of spiritual homelessness.

This study calls for urgent recognition of spiritual abuse as a legitimate and deeply impactful form of trauma. It reveals how the evangelical system—when rigid, fear-based, and performance-oriented—harms the very essence of a person: their connection to Self, to others, and to the Divine.

As faith deconstruction becomes an increasingly visible movement, this research provides a foundational understanding of the psychological and developmental implications of leaving, or healing from, abusive religious systems. It also challenges mental health professionals, spiritual caregivers, and faith leaders to expand their frameworks, deepen their compassion, and begin holding space for the sacred work of soul restoration.

Above all, this research affirms what so many have longed to hear:

You are not alone.
You are not crazy.
You are a Beautiful Soul, Deeply Loved.

And your healing is holy.

6

Coming Home to Yourself

"The privilege of a lifetime is to become who you truly are."

—CARL JUNG

This phenomenological study revealed a deep and devastating truth—there is great harm being done within the evangelical Christian church through the enforcement of dogmatic doctrines, toxic teachings, and spiritual authority misused as control. The data confirmed what many have only sensed in silence: that these practices wound the Soul. They distort one's relationship with the Self, with others, and with the Divine.

Dr. James Fowler reminds us that faith is a living, evolving process. It is not a static creed to be memorized, nor a rigid structure to be conformed to. Faith is born of story, of symbols and sacred rituals, and above all, of one's unique unfolding experience with meaning and mystery.[1] It is a dynamic and transformative pattern that helps the Soul make sense of life. Transitions in faith, therefore, are not signs of failure, they are sacred invitations. When communities recognize this, they become sanctuaries of growth. When they do not, they become systems of harm.

What emerged from this study is that the evangelical religious system obstructs this natural evolution. It arrests the journey of faith development and punishes those who dare to grow. The very disruption required for one to transition into a deeper stage of faith is pathologized, ridiculed, or condemned. Participants in this study suffered not because they were lost, but because they were brave enough to seek.

At the heart of this abuse lies shame. Toxic shame, as perpetuated in evangelical doctrine, convinces the soul it is inherently defective, depraved, and unworthy of love. This shame is not merely psychological, it is spiritual. It severs access to the sacred center of one's being, the indwelling place where the soul communes with the Divine. It shatters the pathway to transcendence.

Nietzsche called such religion a "slave religion"—one that strips power from the individual, rewarding obedience over authenticity. While Nietzsche rejected institutional religion, he revered Jesus as the exemplar of the awakened, sovereign Soul—what he called the *Übermensch*, or Higher Self. He believed the Church twisted the message of Jesus into a doctrine of fear, guilt, and blind conformity. Convictions, Nietzsche warned, are more dangerous than lies, for they close the door to inquiry, insight, and peace.[1]

Kierkegaard, too, was a fierce critic of institutionalized religion. Yet his heart remained devoted to Christ. He believed that faith must be a *lived* experience—not a mental assent, but a Soul encounter. Spiritual truth, Kierkegaard argued, cannot be inherited or imposed. It must be chosen, felt, risked. For him, the most meaningful relationship a person could have was not with a church, but with God—and it must be entered through the free, trembling leap of the heart.[2]

Carl Jung spoke of another leap: the journey of individuation. He believed the purpose of life was to become whole—to integrate the fragmented aspects of self into a conscious, unified Being. But this cannot happen in systems that reward suppression over integration. Jung knew that true transformation comes only by facing what lies within, even the contradictions, and allowing the unconscious to come into the light.[2]

In this way, Fowler, Nietzsche, Kierkegaard, and Jung all point to the same spiritual truth: that we are meant to *become*. We are meant to grow, to question, to unfold. And we are meant to do so in relationship with the Divine—not through rigid conformity, but through Soul freedom. Yet the findings of this study show that those caught in the rigid structure of the evangelical church are denied this very freedom. They are denied the dignity of becoming.

Participants in this study were not lost, they were awakening. But in systems that confuse awakening with rebellion, such individuals are ostracized, gaslit, and shamed. The road to deeper faith is misrepresented as sin. The search for authenticity is labeled heresy. The desire to grow becomes a sentence to isolation.

This is what Jesus named when He said in Matthew 7:13,

"Narrow is the gate and difficult is the way which leads to life, and there are few who find it."

It is not narrow because it is exclusive. It is narrow because it is brave. Because it is sacred. Because few will risk deconstructing the self they were told they *had* to be in order to discover the soul they were *born to become*.

This journey of reexamination, grief, and spiritual courage is the road less traveled. But it is also the road that leads to life. True life. Whole life. The life of the Soul—Deeply Known, Deeply Seen, and Deeply Loved.

Part Three Summary

The Inner Architecture of Understanding:
A Sacred Invitation to the Research

This section illuminated the profound psychological and spiritual harm caused by rigid doctrines, toxic teachings, and the misuse of authority within the evangelical Christian church. The findings reveal how this system inhibits natural spiritual evolution, arresting individuals in immature stages of faith development, as outlined by Dr. James Fowler. Rather than nurturing the Soul's sacred journey through the disruption and transformation that foster growth, evangelicalism often pathologizes this process—trapping believers in fear, shame, and disconnection from their True Selves.

Faith, as Fowler so eloquently describes, is not static but a dynamic, evolving pattern of seeking meaning, value, and identity. Yet in the evangelical system, questioning is forbidden, doubt is condemned, and divergence is met with punishment. This leaves individuals spiritually immobilized, unable to integrate their inner conflicts or advance toward individuation.

The philosophical critiques of thinkers like Friedrich Nietzsche underscore this dilemma. Nietzsche condemned institutional religion for promoting dependence, immaturity, and toxic moral absolutism. He believed convictions—unquestionable beliefs held in the name of truth—were more dangerous than lies, and that humanity must reclaim its right to meaning-making from within. Søren Kierkegaard, while a devout Christian, echoed this in his call for a deeply personal, emotional, and experiential relationship with God—one that transcends dogma and requires the courage of a "leap of faith." He believed that faith must be lived, not legislated.

Psychologist Carl Jung similarly taught that the goal of life is individuation—the integration of all aspects of the self into wholeness. This transformative process, which requires the freedom to explore one's unconscious and inner knowing, cannot occur in systems that demand suppression and conformity. The evangelical church's rigidity obstructs this sacred psychological and spiritual process, leaving many fragmented, spiritually homeless, and disconnected from their inner compass.

Ultimately, this research calls for a courageous reevaluation of the evangelical church's teachings. It advocates for a spiritual path that encourages authentic growth, inner integration, and the unfolding of the individual's relationship with the Divine. It invites us to release fear-based control and rediscover the sacred rhythm of personal transformation. Healing from spiritual abuse is not merely about recovery—it is about reclaiming one's right to evolve, to connect with Love, and to become fully who you were always meant to be.

PART FOUR

Reclaiming the Heart of Faith: Challenging Toxic Teachings and Rediscovering Love

Part Four

This final section is for those of you who are ready—perhaps for the first time—to gently but bravely question the foundational tenets of evangelicalism. It is for those who sense, deep within, that something about what they were taught does not fully align with the Love they once believed in, the peace they long for, or the Jesus they once knew.

You may be surprised to discover that many of the doctrines you've been taught—doctrines attributed to Jesus—are not what He actually taught. You've likely been told that these dogmas are ancient truths, unchanged since Jesus walked the earth over 2,000 years ago. But as you begin to peel back the layers, you may come to see that many of these teachings were never His to begin with.

The invitation here is simple but powerful:

Until we give ourselves permission to question,
we may never find the Truth.

The teachings of Jesus are Divine. They are rooted in Love. They bear fruit that nourishes the Soul, heals the brokenhearted, and leads us toward peace and the eternal presence of Life. But not everything said in His name reflects His heart. The evangelical system has often veiled Jesus behind fear, control, and distortion. And it is time to remove that veil.

WHERE DO WE BEGIN?

Begin with curiosity. Begin with your own questions. Begin by listening to the whisper within that says, *there must be more than this.*

What follows is simply a starting point—a doorway. I encourage you not to stop here...

Read.

Explore.

Ask.

Wrestle.

Wonder.

Let this be the sacred beginning of your path to spiritual freedom.

You were never meant to walk someone else's path. The journey back to your Soul will be as unique as your fingerprint. Trust your intuition. Follow your own sacred knowing. If you listen deeply, you will hear. And if you keep walking, the path will unfold.

Jesus once said, *"The Kingdom of God is within you."*

That is where this journey begins—and where it will lead you home.

7

Through the Lens of Love: Challenging What We Were Taught

"What comes into our minds when we think about God is the most important thing about us."

—A.W. TOZER

Let us begin with a sacred pause—a breath of permission to question.
If you were raised in the evangelical Christian subculture, you likely believed that the four Gospels—Matthew, Mark, Luke, and John—were written by Jesus' closest disciples, those who followed Him, broke bread with Him, and bore witness to His ministry firsthand.

But what if that's not the full story?

What if the teachings you've been told were directly from Jesus... weren't actually His at all?

What if buried beneath centuries of hierarchy, empire, and control, there lies a truer Gospel—one that was silenced but not extinguished?

This chapter is not about destroying faith—it is about liberating it.

It is about honoring Jesus enough to ask, *"What did He really say?"*
And what was added later... in His name?

THE CREATION OF THE CANON

The Bible, as we know it today, did not fall from the sky. It was not compiled by Jesus or His original followers. It wasn't even fully assembled for more than 300 years after His death.

In 325 CE, Emperor Constantine of Rome convened the Council of Nicaea—the first ecumenical council of the Christian Church. Before this point, Christians had been severely persecuted. But Constantine, seeing the unifying power of religion, made Christianity the official religion of the empire.

He wanted unity—not just spiritually, but politically. So, he demanded that over 300 bishops come to consensus on "correct" Christian belief. The result was the Nicene Creed, and from it emerged what we now call orthodoxy. Those who did not agree were deemed heretics. Their texts were banned, their communities dissolved, their teachings destroyed.[1,2]

From this decree came the Biblical Canon—the official collection of books allowed to be read and followed. Many other writings, some of which may have captured the voice and teachings of Jesus more directly, were excluded, burned, or hidden.

The four Gospels that were chosen—Matthew, Mark, Luke, and John—were written 40 to 70 years after Jesus' death. They were not authored by those who walked with Him. Scholars agree: these were not eyewitness accounts. The original disciples were Aramaic-speaking Jews of humble origin. The Gospels, however, were written in Greek—by educated individuals living in different regions and generations.[1,2,3]

WHAT WAS LOST?

If these Gospels were chosen to align with the empire's version of Jesus, what voices were silenced?

In 1945, an extraordinary discovery was made in Nag Hammadi, Egypt: a library of ancient Christian texts that had been hidden for centuries. These Nag Hammadi codices, alongside the Dead Sea

Scrolls found in Qumran, reveal a vibrant, mystical, and deeply diverse landscape of early Christianity.[1,2,4]

Among them is the *Gospel of Thomas*—a collection of Jesus' sayings that emphasize inner knowing, divine union, and the Kingdom of God *within*. This text doesn't focus on Jesus' death or resurrection. Instead, it centers on His message of awakening, transformation, and soul-deep liberation.[1,4,5]

According to the *Biblical Archaeology Society* (2024):

"Among the Nag Hammadi texts was the fully preserved *Gospel of Thomas*, which does not follow the canonical Gospels in telling the story of Jesus' birth, life, crucifixion, and resurrection, but rather presents the reader with an early collection of Jesus' sayings. Although this mystical text was originally believed to be one of the early texts of Gnosticism, it now seems to reveal yet another strand of early Christianity. From a historical perspective, the Nag Hammadi codices provide a clearer picture of the diverse theological and philosophical currents that found expression through early Christianity. Indeed, Gnosticism and its classically inspired philosophical ideals permeated not just early Christian thought but also the Jewish and pagan traditions from which Christianity arose. The Nag Hammadi codices, widely regarded as one of the most significant finds of the 20th century, revealed this complex religious milieu and offered an unparalleled glimpse into alternative visions of early Christianity."

Before Christianity was defined by hierarchy, orthodoxy, and control, it was known as *The Way*—a path of love, humility, communal living, and spiritual transformation. It was non-institutional. It was experiential. It was alive.

Groups like the Ebionites emphasized Jesus' humanity. The Gnostics taught about Divine wisdom and the Soul's inner journey. There was no single "correct" Christianity—there were many expressions, all centered around the mystery and presence of Christ.[1,4,5]

But as the Roman Empire consolidated power, these expressions were silenced. What was deemed *heretical* often had little to do with truth—and everything to do with control.

THE LOST HEART OF JESUS

When we look at the teachings of Jesus with clear eyes and an open heart, we find a radically inclusive message—a vision of Divine Love, not divine punishment.

His call was to Love, not legalism.
To humility, not hierarchy.
To healing, not control.
To inner transformation, not external performance.

But when church and empire merged, these teachings were systematized into dogma. Jesus' message became co-opted by power, and over time, the institutional church bore less resemblance to His life and more to the very structures He challenged.

WHY THIS MATTERS NOW

Understanding the historical roots of evangelicalism and the canonization of Scripture is not about discrediting Jesus, it is about honoring Him. It is about reclaiming the Truth that was buried beneath centuries of fear-based theology and empire-building.

This is not a rejection of God.
It is a rejection of distortion.
And it is the beginning of healing.

Let this chapter be your permission slip—to question, to seek, to *remember*. You are not walking away from Jesus. You are walking with Him.

You are stepping into the light of what He really taught.
You are stepping into *The Way*, again.

CHAPTER 7 SUMMARY
Through the Lens of Love: Challenging What We Were Taught

This chapter invites you to peel back the layers of history and rediscover Jesus beyond the constraints of institutional theology—reclaiming the story of Jesus. By exploring how the Bible was shaped and whose voices were silenced, we reclaim the spiritual depth, diversity, and beauty of early Christian wisdom. In honoring what was lost, we remember what Love has always been: inclusive, unbounded, and free.

8

Reclaiming Your Truth

"The greatest gift is not being afraid to question."

—RUBY DEE

For many, the evangelical path offers certainty—a sense of belonging, clear rules, and the comfort of knowing where one stands. But for others, especially those who have suffered under its more damaging doctrines, that same certainty becomes a cage.

What once felt like spiritual guidance can become psychological, emotional, and spiritual imprisonment.

This chapter is for those brave enough to peer beyond that cage.

Here, we will explore how evangelical doctrine has been shaped—not solely by Divine inspiration, but by power, politics, and human interpretation. Together, we'll begin to unravel the complexities behind what many have been told is "truth" and gently question the roots of spiritual beliefs that have caused harm.

THE COURAGE TO QUESTION

To question is not to betray your faith, it is to deepen it. It is to listen to the still, small voice within that says, *"This doesn't feel like Love."*

Through the lens of scholars such as Dr. Elaine Pagels, Dr. Michael Heiser, Dr. David Bentley Hart, Dr. Bart Ehrman, and Dr. Eitan Bar, we will step into a more expansive understanding of early Christianity, the Bible, and the doctrines that have shaped modern evangelical thought.

Dr. Elaine Pagels (1943–) an author and Professor at Columbia University until her appointment of Professor of Early Christian History at Princeton University for forty-two years. She is best known for her research and publication involving translating ancient Greek texts from the Egyptian Coptic texts of the Nag Hammadi codices. She received her PhD from Harvard University.

Dr. Michael Heiser (1963–2023) was an American Old Testament scholar and author. He was an expert in the Bible and ancient Semitic languages who earned a PhD in Hebrew Bible and Semitic languages.

Dr. David Bentley Hart (1965–) an Orthodox theologian, author, Philosopher, and religious studies scholar. He achieved his MPhil in Theology at Cambridge University and his PhD in Religious Studies at the University of Virginia.

Dr. Bart Ehrman (1955–) an expert on the New Testament and history of Early Christianity. He is a Professor at the University of North Carolina at Chapel Hill. He completed his MDiv and PhD at Princeton Seminary. He is a six times *New York Times* Bestseller with one of his books titled *Misquoting Jesus*.

Dr. Eitan Bar (1984–) a Theologian, author, and scholar. Born and raised in Israel and native Hebrew speaker, he combines his Jewish heritage with his Biblical scholarship to offer new and timely perspectives on Christianity.

These respected voices in theological and historical research—each with years of study in early Christian history, Semitic languages, textual criticism, and Biblical archaeology—offer clarity where confusion has reigned and open doors where gatekeepers once stood.

Let us explore the core tenants of evangelical belief…

DOCTRINE OF THE INERRANCY OF THE BIBLE

Reclaiming Sacred Wisdom: Reading the Bible with Freedom and Love

A Constructed Canon: The Bible's Complicated Origin

If you were raised to believe that the Bible is the literal, perfect Word of God, you are not alone. Evangelicalism often teaches that the Bible is inerrant—without error, timeless, and unchangeable in all matters of faith and practice.

But here's what many have never been told:

- The Bible was not formed overnight.
- Jesus never handed it down.
- And for more than three centuries after His death, there *was no official Bible.*

In 325 CE, under Emperor Constantine's leadership, the Roman Empire convened the Council of Nicaea to settle theological disputes and unify Christian belief. This was not a spiritual gathering alone—it was also a political maneuver to stabilize a fragmented empire.

At this council, bishops debated, defined, and ultimately enforced what would become "orthodox" Christian doctrine. Those who disagreed were labeled heretics, and their writings—many of which reflected alternative perspectives of Jesus' teachings—were burned or banned. From these decisions, the Biblical Canon was born.[1,2]

The Gospels of Matthew, Mark, Luke, and John were written 40 to 70 years after Jesus' death—in Greek, not Aramaic, by educated authors who were likely not among Jesus' original followers. Most scholars agree: the disciples did not write the Gospels. Yet, these texts were chosen to align with a singular theological narrative—one shaped more by unity and control than by the full breadth of early Christian experience.[1,2,3]

What Was Left Out?

Have you ever wondered what else was once believed? What other stories were told by those who *did* walk with Jesus?

Ancient texts unearthed in Nag Hammadi, Egypt (1945) and the Qumran caves (1946–1956) offer us answers. These discoveries, which include the *Gospel of Thomas* and the *Gospel of Mary*, reveal a Christianity that was more mystical, inner-focused, and non-hierarchical. A Christianity that taught the *Kingdom of God is within*, and that Divine wisdom lives in each Soul.[1,4,5]

Rather than emphasizing dogma, these texts highlight:

- *Transformation*, not control.
- *Union with the Divine*, not separation.
- *Knowing yourself*, not shame.

As Dr. Elaine Pagels and many others have shown, these texts were not fringe—they were vibrant expressions of early Christian faith.[1,6] They were silenced not because they lacked truth, but because they did not fit the power structures forming at the time.

Challenging Inerrancy with Integrity

Dr. Michael Heiser reminds us that Scripture is not a flat, literal document. It is layered, ancient, and deeply contextual—written by humans within cultures very different from our own. To interpret it without nuance is to risk distorting its message. Literal readings of Genesis, demonology, or end-times prophecy often reflect more about modern bias than ancient wisdom.[7]

When we recognize that the Bible was shaped by human hands, political needs, and historical circumstances, we are not "losing faith"—we are gaining a more truthful, Spirit-led relationship with it. This doesn't diminish its sacred value; it restores it to a place of reverent curiosity, not blind obedience.

The Power of What Was Suppressed

The exclusion of texts like the *Gospel of Mary* and teachings from groups such as the Essenes reminds us: spiritual history is not a straight line. Early Christianity held many paths, many expressions of devotion. What we now call "heresy" was once someone's lived, faithful experience of the Divine.[1,2,4]

The early followers of Jesus, those known as *The Way*, lived in communal humility, emphasized inner transformation, and walked with a God who was close, not distant. Their way of life reflected a deep reverence for spiritual freedom and the innate dignity of every Soul.

This is the way of Jesus that your heart may have known before your mind was taught to fear.

An Invitation Forward

Questioning inerrancy is not about rebellion.

It's about *returning*—to Jesus.

To the Love that never required you to earn it.

To the Wisdom that can never be contained in a single book or institution.

The story of faith is far older and deeper than we've been told.

And it is *still unfolding*—within you.

DOCTRINE OF ORIGINAL SIN

*Reclaiming the Goodness
That Was Always Ours*

The doctrine of original sin, introduced by Augustine of Hippo in the fourth century, has profoundly shaped Christian theology—and for many, their personal sense of worth. But it is crucial to remember: *this doctrine did not exist in Christian teaching before Augustine.* And it is equally vital to approach it now with compassion, courage, and a commitment to truth.[1]

This teaching tells us that we are born guilty—that because of the first humans' mistake, we are inherently sinful, separated from God, and worthy of divine punishment. For centuries, this doctrine has created deep grooves of shame, fear, and self-rejection in the hearts of believers who long only to be close to God.

But what if this isn't the whole story?

The Truth That Came First: "Very Good"

Before the fall... there was blessing.
Genesis begins with a resounding affirmation:

> "God saw all that He had made, and it was very good."
>
> —GENESIS 1:31

Humanity was created in the image of God, not in the image of sin. This foundational truth calls us back to our original design—not one of depravity, but of Divine beauty and sacred worth.

The notion that we are born stained, broken, or cursed distorts this original blessing. It turns the Gospel from an invitation into Love into a desperate attempt to escape condemnation.

Where the Doctrine Went Wrong

The story of Adam and Eve in Genesis is a deeply symbolic narrative. While it depicts disobedience and the consequences of human choices, it does not say that all future humans are born guilty of Adam's sin.[2,4]

In Romans 5:12, the Apostle Paul writes,

> *"Therefore, just as sin entered the world through one man, and death through sin, and in this way death came to all people, because all sinned."*

Dr. Eitan Bar, a Bible scholar and theologian, points out that Augustine's Latin rendering of this passage introduced a shift in interpretation. Augustine changed *"because all sinned"* into *"in whom all sinned,"* implying inherited guilt—that all of humanity sinned in Adam. This single shift in interpretation became the foundation for the doctrine of original sin, leading to the widespread belief that all are born condemned.[3.8]

But Paul's original words do not imply inherited guilt—they speak to the reality of human choice, and the ripple effects of brokenness in a fallen world.

What About Free Will?

The doctrine of original sin suggests that we are incapable of choosing good without Divine intervention—that we are trapped in sin, incapable of righteousness, helpless from birth.

But the Bible speaks a different word. In Deuteronomy 30:19, God says:

> *"I have set before you life and death, blessing and cursing; therefore choose life, that both you and your decendants may live."*

Choice is sacred. Agency is divine. God gives us the power to choose Love, to choose Truth, to choose relationship with Him.

What the Cross Really Means

The evangelical interpretation of original sin often teaches that we are so wicked that only Jesus' blood can cover our worthlessness. But this contradicts the very heart of the Gospel.

> "As through one man's offense judgment came to all men, resulting in condemnation, even so through one Man's righteous act the free gift came to all men, resulting in justification of life."
>
> —ROMANS 5:18

This verse speaks not of damnation, but of universal grace. The life, death, and resurrection of Christ offer restoration and belonging to *all*. His message was not "You are guilty"—it was "You are Loved."

Augustine or Irenaeus? Two Views of Humanity

While Augustine painted humanity as fallen and depraved, Irenaeus, a much earlier Church Father, saw things differently. He described humanity not as ruined, but as *growing*. He believed that Adam and Eve were like spiritual children—immature, but not evil—and that the fall was part of the process of learning, evolving, and drawing closer to God.[2,4]

This reframing shifts the narrative from condemnation to compassion. We are not enemies of God from birth—we are divine children growing into the fullness of our being.

Returning to a God Who Is Love

Dr. Bar reminds us that inserting personal bias or fear-based theology into Scripture is called eisegesis—reading into the text what we already believe. He names the doctrine of original sin as one of the clearest examples of this. It has shaped generations of Christians to live in fear, not freedom.[7,8]

> To question this doctrine is not to rebel against God.
> It is to *come home* to Him.
>
> It is to say:
>
> > "I was not created unworthy. I was created in Love.
> > And I am still held in that Love."

A Faith That Heals, Not Harms

When we shed the belief that we are fundamentally flawed, something sacred emerges. We stop striving to *earn* God's Love and begin to *receive* it. We stop hiding in shame and start showing up in truth. We move from fear of punishment to the joy of connection.

This is the heart of the Gospel.

You are not born bad.
You are not separated.
You are not unworthy.
You are a Beautiful Soul, Deeply Loved.

And the return to that truth is the beginning of everything.

DOCTRINE OF ETERNAL CONSCIOUS TORMENT

Reclaiming the God of Love from the Theology of Fear

Few doctrines have inflicted more fear, anxiety, and spiritual paralysis than the belief in eternal conscious torment—a literal, unending hell where souls are punished forever for their shortcomings in this life. This theology has deeply shaped the evangelical imagination and, in doing so, distorted the nature of God, the message of Jesus, and the very essence of Love.

To question this doctrine is not to rebel.
It is to return to the truth that *God is Love.*

The Psychological Toll of a Fear-Based Theology

For those raised under this teaching, the emotional cost can be devastating. The thought of unending torment fosters not reverence, but terror: a belief that you must earn God's love, that one wrong move could cost you eternity, and that your inherent worth is contingent on perfection. Many live with a haunting fear of *"being left behind,"* burdened with guilt for not saving others, and silently wondering if they will ever be *"good enough."*

This fear does not lead to freedom.
It fractures the soul.

A Doctrine That Didn't Begin with Jesus

Dr. Bart Ehrman, a preeminent scholar of early Christianity, reminds us that the idea of eternal punishment was not taught by Jesus, nor was it present in the earliest Christian writings. The Hebrew Scriptures spoke of *Sheol*—a shadowy, indistinct afterlife. The Greek-influenced concept of *Hades* was more symbolic than punitive. Neither resembled the fiery torment described in later Christian theology.

The graphic vision of hell that dominates evangelical preaching today took root *centuries after Jesus,* shaped by cultural anxiety, political consolidation, and theologians such as Augustine, who introduced harsh doctrines of inherited guilt and punishment.[2,3]

It was not the Christ of Love who conceived of hell as eternal torture.

It was the Church that codified fear to control belief.

Jesus' Message Was Always About Love

Jesus never wielded fear as a weapon. He healed the outcast, embraced the outsider, and forgave the condemned. His parables pointed to transformation, not torment. His message was one of *reconciliation*—that God's desire is not to punish, but to restore.

> "Love your enemies, do good, and lend, hoping for nothing in return; and your reward will be great, and you will be sons of the Most High. For He is kind to the unthankful and evil. Therefore, be merciful, just as your Father is merciful."
>
> —LUKE 6:35-36

When we project eternal punishment onto God, we make Him smaller than the Love He sent into the world through Christ. We substitute *eternal fear* for *eternal grace*.

A God Who Desires All to Be Saved

Scripture is filled with hope for all humanity:

> "[God] who desires all men to be saved and to come to the knowledge of the truth."
>
> —1 TIMOTHY 2:4

> "The Lord is merciful and gracious, slow to anger, abounding in mercy. He will not always strive with us, nor will He keep His anger forever."
>
> —PSALM 103:8–9

If God's deepest desire is reconciliation, how can we believe He would condemn billions to unending suffering? Would a loving parent ever choose eternal punishment for a child who didn't understand?

Dr. David Bentley Hart, in his profound work *That All Shall Be Saved*, writes that eternal punishment is utterly incompatible with Divine goodness. No finite act could warrant infinite torment. He calls the doctrine of eternal hell not only theologically indefensible, but morally appalling.[9]

What Scripture Actually Says

The word "hell" in most Bibles is often translated from the term *Gehenna*—a valley outside Jerusalem once associated with idolatry and child sacrifice, later used as a metaphor for destruction. Jesus used it as a symbolic warning—not to describe an eternal torture chamber, but to highlight the gravity of unloving actions.[3,10]

The parables of judgment are best understood through the lens of transformation, not retribution. Jesus warned of consequences for injustice, hypocrisy, and cruelty—but He always offered redemption.

Hell, when interpreted through historical and linguistic context, does not hold up as a doctrine of eternal, conscious torment.

What it does offer is an invitation to rethink what justice, love, and mercy really mean.

The Early Church Did Not All Agree

Many early Church Fathers—including Origen, Gregory of Nyssa, and Clement of Alexandria—affirmed the idea of universal reconciliation: that all souls would eventually be restored to God. Their vision of salvation was rooted not in fear, but in the unending reach of God's grace.[2,3,9]

It was only through the consolidation of Church power that this diversity of belief was suppressed. Once again, what was labeled *heresy* was often simply *hope*.

A Theology That Heals, Not Harms

To challenge the doctrine of eternal torment is not to deny the seriousness of sin or the reality of justice. Rather, it is to believe that justice, when truly Divine, is *restorative*—not retributive. It is to believe in a God who mends what is broken, who leaves the ninety-nine to find the one, who never stops seeking until all are gathered into Love.

By leaving behind the theology of fear, we step into *a theology of wholeness*.

We embrace:

- Accountability without condemnation.
- Repentance without shame.
- Grace without conditions.
- Love without end.

An Invitation to Remember

If the doctrine of hell has caused you to live in fear, to question your worth, or to tremble at the thought of God—know this:

You were never meant to be afraid of Love.

You were created to walk with the Divine, not run from Him.

To receive grace, not earn it.

To trust, not to tremble.

Let this be your permission to breathe again.

To question. To learn.

To come home to the God whose Love never fails, and never ends.

DOCTRINE OF CONVERSION

*Reclaiming the Power of Love
from the Theology of Transaction*

The Need for Substitutionary Atonement?

The Cross stands at the heart of Christian faith. But what has it come to symbolize?

For many raised in evangelical Christianity, the answer is this: Jesus died in your place to pay for your sin. This belief, rooted in penal substitutionary atonement, teaches that humanity's sin incurred Divine wrath, and the only way God could forgive was through a violent sacrifice—punishing Jesus instead of us.[2,8]

But what if this is not the whole story?

What if this interpretation, while earnest in its attempt to understand the mystery of the Cross, has missed the deeper truth?

A Doctrine Born of Blood, Not of the Beatitudes

The penal substitution model, which portrays God as a wrathful judge requiring blood to satisfy justice, was *not* the central message of early Christianity. As Dr. Elaine Pagels notes in her translation of early Christian texts, many first-century believers centered their hope not on Jesus' death, but on His resurrection—His victory over death, His embodiment of Divine Love, and His promise of new life.[2,4,5]

This idea of a violent transaction to appease an angry God emerged later—an inheritance not from Jesus' teachings, but from pagan sacrificial systems and a legal framework that emphasized guilt and punishment over restoration and grace.[3,8]

To center the Cross around punishment is to miss what Jesus revealed with every breath He took:

That *Love is the only thing that saves.*

A Gospel Rooted in Fear, or in Freedom?

When penal substitution becomes the heart of the Gospel, it leads to a God who must be appeased. Believers are taught they are inherently wicked, and unless they "accept Jesus" as the substitute for their deserved punishment, they are doomed to eternal separation.

But this theology does not reflect the heart of the One who said:

"Neither do I condemn you."

"Love your enemies."

"Be merciful, just as your Father is merciful."

Instead, it creates a transactional faith based on anxiety and guilt—where salvation is something to secure, rather than a relationship to receive. It keeps the believer in a perpetual loop of not being enough.

God Is Not a Divine Accountant

If God's Love must first be satisfied by blood, is it truly unconditional?
1 John 4:8 says clearly:

"He who does not love does not know God, for God is Love."

Not *anger* balanced by love. Not *justice* requiring violence. Just **Love**.
This Love is not conditional upon punishment.
This Love does not need to be bought.
This Love simply **IS**.

"God was in Christ reconciling the world to Himself, not imputing their trespasses to them, and has committed to us the word of reconciliation."

—2 CORINTHIANS 5:19

This is not a God who demanded a payment.
This is a God who came to heal what was broken.

Alternative Visions of the Cross

Love Poured Out, Not Wrath Diverted

Jesus' words in John 15:13 are a tender reframing:

"Greater love has no one than this, than to lay down one's life for his friends."

What if the cross is not about punishment, but *presence*?

Not God's wrath unleashed, but *God's love poured out*?

Not a substitute, but a *solidarity*?

In this view, the cross becomes the *ultimate act of Divine compassion*. Jesus entered our suffering not to satisfy a demand, but to say: *You are not alone.*

Christus Victor: The Triumph of Love

Another ancient view, Christus Victor, presents the cross and resurrection as God's cosmic victory over sin, death, and all that separates us from Love. In this view, Jesus didn't die to appease an angry Father, but to break the chains of everything that binds us.[2]

> "He has made alive together with Him, having forgiven you all trespasses, having wiped out the handwriting of requirements that was against us, which was contrary to us. And He has taken it out of the way, having nailed it to the cross. Having disarmed principalities and powers, He made a public spectacle of them, triumphing over them in it."
>
> —COLOSSIANS 2:13-15

The cross is not the end of the story. It's the opening of a new world.

Jesus Did Not Die to Change God's Mind About Us

He died to *show us* what God has always been like.

In Christ, we do not see a Father demanding a blood price. We see the fullness of God's heart: a Love that heals, that forgives, that walks with us even into death—and through it.

Jesus did not come to secure our worth.

He came to remind us that we already have it.

A Love that Restores, Not Condemns

Early Christian voices like Irenaeus emphasized the restorative power of Christ—not punishment, but healing. Jesus came to restore the image of God within us, to reawaken what had been forgotten: that we are already deeply loved, already worthy, already held in the arms of grace.[2,4]

This message is not one of wrath. It is one of *homecoming*.

A New Vision for Faith

To move beyond penal substitution is not to discard the Cross, it is to reclaim it.

To see it not as a divine transaction, but as a love letter in scarlet ink.

To follow not a gospel of fear, but a gospel of freedom.

Let this truth sink in:

You were never meant to pay for being human.

*You were meant to be held in **Love**.*

CHAPTER 8 SUMMARY
Reclaiming Your Truth

In this chapter, we tenderly examine the doctrines that have caused the greatest harm—biblical inerrancy, original sin, hell, and substitutionary atonement—not to destroy faith, but to liberate it. With the help of scholars and the wisdom of Spirit, we invite a return to the Gospel of Love, healing, and mercy—reclaiming the *heart* of the Gospel. This is a call to trust what your heart has always known: that you are already worthy, and that Love does not require fear to be true.

Part Four Summary

Reclaiming the Heart of Faith:
Challenging Toxic Teachings and Rediscovering Love

In this final section, we engaged with some of the most central tenets of evangelical theology—not to tear down faith, but to liberate it from fear-based distortions and restore it to the realm of love, freedom, and truth. Drawing upon the wisdom of scholars such as Dr. Elaine Pagels, Dr. Michael Heiser, Dr. David Bentley Hart, Dr. Bart Ehrman, and Dr. Eitan Bar, we explored how these doctrines were shaped—often not by Jesus' teachings—but by historical power structures, theological agendas, and institutional control.

We questioned not God, but the *narratives that have obscured the God of Love*.

THE DOCTRINE OF BIBLICAL INERRANCY

The belief that the Bible is the literal and infallible Word of God has become a cornerstone of evangelicalism. Yet, the canonization of scripture was shaped by imperial politics and theological disputes, not divine dictation.

As Dr. Michael Heiser and others reveal, the Bible is a divinely inspired yet deeply human collection of writings, written across centuries, in multiple languages, and within complex cultural contexts.

To insist on a rigid, literal inerrancy is to miss the richness of its wisdom, and to turn the Living Word into a *rulebook*.

THE DOCTRINE OF ORIGINAL SIN

Augustine's interpretation of Romans 5:12 gave rise to the belief that every soul is born guilty—a theology that has haunted hearts with shame and spiritual paralysis for over 1,500 years. Dr. Eitan Bar's work points to a critical mistranslation that shifted the meaning from "because all sinned" to "in whom all sinned," birthing the idea of inherited guilt.

Theological interpretations also come into question. This research contrasts the punitive, guilt-centered doctrine of Augustine with the more compassionate and growth-oriented view of Irenaeus, who saw the fall of humanity not as a moral failure, but as part of a maturing process. Had the church embraced this understanding, it may have fostered a doctrine of Love rather than fear, and a theology that honors the unfolding journey of the Soul.

By reclaiming the truth of humanity's original goodness, free will, and the redemptive embrace of Christ, we are reminded:

You were never meant to be condemned.
You were always meant to be *loved*.

THE DOCTRINE OF ETERNAL CONSCIOUS TORMENT

The evangelical image of Hell, a place of unending torture, is not found in the teachings of Jesus or the early church.

As Dr. Bart Ehrman and Dr. David Bentley Hart have shown, this doctrine evolved over time, shaped more by fear, control, and cultural mythology than by the message of Christ. Instead of terrorizing people into faith, Jesus invites us into union through Love. Alternatives like universal reconciliation or restorative justice echo the deeper truth:

God desires *healing*, not torment.
Relationship, not retribution.

THE DOCTRINE OF PENAL SUBSTITUTIONARY ATONEMENT

This theory, where Jesus' death is framed as a Divine payment to satisfy God's wrath, turns the Cross into a transaction.

But scholars like Dr. Pagels and theologians like Dr. Hart remind us: this was not the only view in early Christianity. In fact, many emphasized the resurrection, healing, and Christus Victor —a victorious overcoming of death and evil, not appeasement through blood.

The Cross was not about punishment.

It was, and still is, *Love made visible.*

Not a God who demands suffering, but a God who walks with us through it, and transforms it into new life.

A WAY FORWARD

This exploration is not an exit from faith—it is an invitation back to its truest center:

*A compassionate, liberating, relational Love
that cannot be earned or revoked.*

Reexamining these doctrines is not betrayal, it is integrity. It is the brave work of healing, growing, and returning to the sacred truth that God is not who we were taught to fear... but who we were created to know.

May this reclaimed vision of faith offer a pathway:

From shame to *belonging*,

From fear to **Love**,

From dogma to *Divine encounter*.

HOME-COMING OF THE SOUL

Awakening to Love, Freedom, and True Self

Stepping into the Light

"The world we see that seems so insane is the result of a belief system that is not working. To perceive the world differently, we must be willing to change our belief system, let the past slip away, expand our sense of now, and dissolve the fear in our minds."

—WILLIAM JAMES

The doctrines of American evangelicalism have caused immense psychological, emotional, and spiritual harm to countless souls. Rooted in fear, guilt, and shame, these teachings distort not only our understanding of God but also our view of self, others, and the world. They create a framework of control—often cloaked in religious language—that severs our innate connection to the Divine and conditions us to distrust our own hearts.

But healing is possible.

When we courageously begin to examine and deconstruct these doctrines, we begin to reclaim our spiritual lives—not by abandoning faith, but by returning it to its origin: **Love**. This journey may involve reinterpreting Scripture, letting go of inherited beliefs, and embracing a broader, more compassionate understanding of spirituality—one that welcomes truth, mystery, and belonging.

Imagine how different the Christian Church might have been if it had adopted the teachings of Irenaeus instead of Augustine.

Irenaeus viewed the Fall not as a catastrophe that separated us from God, but as an act of human immaturity—the first painful step into self-awareness. He believed that the redemption of humanity did not require the violent crucifixion of an innocent Christ to appease Divine wrath. Instead, Irenaeus proposed that Christ lovingly recapitulated our journey, walking with us from our immaturity toward our full maturation in the image of God.

This vision is healing. It is hopeful. It is rooted in Divine solidarity, not punishment.

Scholars like Dr. Elaine Pagels, Dr. Eitan Bar, Dr. Michael Heiser, Dr. David Bentley Hart, and Dr. Bart Ehrman provide an invaluable pathway toward liberation. Through their work, we rediscover that there were many voices in early Christianity—many paths, many perspectives—and that the one we were taught in evangelicalism is *not the only one*. Their scholarship empowers us to question not out of rebellion, but out of reverence—for God, for Truth, and for our own healing.

Through this lens, the teachings of Jesus become clearer: not a God of wrath demanding blood, but a *God of Radical Love*—One who lifts up the lowly, dines with the outcast, and breaks bread across lines of exclusion. Jesus reveals a Love that liberates, that restores, that welcomes the questions... because *Truth is never threatened by inquiry.*

To step into the light is not to abandon faith, but to shed the layers of fear that have distorted it.

This new paradigm of faith is not about rejecting the sacred, it is about reclaiming it. It is about building a faith that is grounded in compassion, shaped by humility, and nourished by inclusivity. It is about restoring what was lost—our right to trust our inner knowing, our birthright to experience spiritual joy, and our sacred invitation to connect with the Divine not through shame, but through intimacy.

This transformation requires more than just changing beliefs— it requires dismantling power structures that silence, oppress, and control. Evangelicalism's hierarchical model, where authority is often placed above discernment, leaves little room for dialogue, nuance, or dissent. But a healthier faith invites us into a circle instead of a ladder—a space where questions are honored, voices are heard, and everyone is welcome.

As Dr. David Bentley Hart has so passionately argued, the gospel is not about eternal punishment, it is about universal Love. It is a message that transcends tribalism, dismantles spiritual elitism, and calls us to something deeper than dogma: it calls us to **be Love**.

If you have felt abandoned, disoriented, or broken by the teachings of evangelicalism—you are not alone. And you are not lost. You are awakening.

You are awakening to the possibility that your pain is not the end of your story but the beginning of your resurrection.

You are *allowed* to question.

You are *allowed* to wrestle.

You are *allowed* to heal.

You are *allowed* to find God not outside of you, but *within*.

Let your questions lead you to deeper communion. Let your doubts become doorways. Let your grief become the sacred ground upon which new truth can take root.

May you find companions on this journey—people and places that honor your questions, celebrate your heart, and reflect the Divine image back to you with tenderness.

Because the truth is this:

You have always belonged. You have always been Loved.

And you are finally *free* to walk in that Light.

A New Beginning

"I am not what happened to me; I am what I choose to become."

—CARL JUNG

It is time.
Time to confront the toxic teachings of American evangelicalism and reclaim the radiant truth of the Gospel—the message of **Love**, of inclusion, of healing. It is time for those who have been spiritually abused to name what has happened, to mourn what has been lost, and to begin again. The journey toward restoration is not easy, but it is sacred. It holds the promise of a future rooted not in fear and control, but in Hope, Peace, and Liberation.

This moment calls to us.

As clinical psychologists, as scholars, as pastors, teachers, parents, friends, and advocates for the soul, we are being invited to walk alongside those who are courageously deconstructing the doctrines that once defined them—and are now reclaiming their own sacred path. We must offer them what they were once denied: validation, space to question, space to feel, and space to heal.

In doing so, we begin to build a future where spiritual abuse has no home—where communities are safe for the questioning, tender toward the brokenhearted, and alive with the presence of God's Love.

I am standing now, on the top of my desk, crying out: "O Captain! My Captain!"

I am standing for those who have been silenced.

I am standing for those who "know not what they do."

I am standing for **Jesus**, the One who embodies Love unbound by doctrine or fear.

I am standing so the truth of His heart may finally be known—free from the damage of dogma, free from the weight of shame.

·······

Will you stand with me?

Will you move from the seat of silent suffering and step onto your own sacred desk?

Will you rise—for the children within us who were never meant to be taught they were unworthy?

Will you rise—for the healing of generations to come?

This is not just the end of an old story.
This is the *beginning* of a *new* one.

A new spiritual awakening is calling; one where Love, Justice, and Truth are not feared, but followed. One where freedom and dignity are not earned through conformity but are honored as birthrights. May we enter the most beautiful journey of all:

The journey of rediscovering Who We Are.

May we have the courage to listen to our inner voice.
To trust our beautiful, unbreakable hearts.
To rise in reverence for the Love that lives within us.
And above all—May we . . .

Remember Who We Truly Are.

Appendix
Interview Questions

INTERVIEW QUESTIONS

Demographic Survey

1. How old are you?
2. What is your gender?
3. How long have you been involved with the evangelical church?
4. Are you currently associated with the evangelical church?
5. How long have you been away from the evangelical church?
6. Do you believe that you have been spiritual abused by others involved in the evangelical church?

RQ1. What types of experiences of spiritual abuse have occurred in the Evangelical subculture of the Christian church in the United States of America?

Interview Question 1: What adverse experiences have you encountered in the evangelical church that you attended?

Interview Question 2: What has been the most difficult aspect of attending an evangelical church for you?

RQ2. Do these experiences of spiritual abuse affect self-trust?

Interview Question 3: How do you relate to the aspect of trusting yourself?

Interview Question 4: What are your struggles (if any) in trusting yourself?

Interview Question 5: How would you describe how you see yourself?

RQ3. What impact does this experience of spiritual abuse have on the coping mechanisms in one's personal life?

Interview Question 6: How do you think these experiences of spiritual abuse have affected you?

Interview Question 7: How do you think these experiences have affected your relationships?

Interview Question 8: How do you cope with being affected by spiritual abuse?

Interview Question 9: How do you feel about religious or spiritual beliefs now?

Interview Question 10: How do you view your relationship with God now?

References

CHAPTER ONE

1 Schimmenti, A., & Caretti, V. (2016). Linking the overwhelming with the unbearable: Developmental trauma, dissociation, and the disconnected self. *Psychoanalytic Psychology, 33*(1), 106-128.

2 Wilkinson, M. (2017). Mind, brain and body. Healing trauma: the way forward. *Journal of Analytical Psychology, 62*(4), 526-543.

3 Navalta, C., McGee, L., & Underwood, L. (2018). Adverse childhood experiences, brain development, and mental health: A call for neurocounseling. *Journal of Mental Health Counseling, 40*(3), 266-278.

4 Teicher, M., & Samson, J. (2016). Annual research review: Enduring neurobiological effects of childhood abuse and neglect. *Journal of Child Psychology and Psychiatry, 57*(3), 241-266.

5 Schauer, M., & Elbert, T. (2010). Dissociation following traumatic stress: Etiology and treatment. *Journal of Psychology, 218*(2), 109-117. doi:10-1027/0044-3409/a000018

6 Ginot, E. (2007). Intersubjectivity and neuroscience: Understanding enactments and their therapeutic significance within emerging paradigms. *Psychoanalytic Psychology, 24*(2), 317-332.

7 Siegel, D. (2001). Toward an interpersonal neurobiology of the developing mind: Attachment relationships, "mindsight," and neural integration. *Infant Mental Health Journal, 22*(1-2), 67-94.

8 Porges, S. & Geller, S. (2014). Therapeutic presence: Neurophysiological mechanisms mediating feeling safe in therapeutic relationships. *Journal of Psychotherapy Integration*, 24(3), 178-192.

9 Miller, R., (2016). Neuroeducation: Integrating brain-based psychoeducation into clinical practice. *Journal of Mental Health Counseling*, 38(2), 103-115.

10 Siegel, D. (2012). *Pocket Guide to Interpersonal Neurobiology: An Integrative Handbook of the Mind*. New York, NY: Norton.

11 Kindsvatter, A. & Geroski, A., (2014). The impact of early life stress on the neurodevelopment of the stress response system. *Journal of Counseling & Development*, 92, 472-480.

12 Ducharme, E. (2017). Best practices in working with complex trauma and dissociative identity disorder. *Practice Innovations*. Advance online publication. http://dx.doi.org/10.1037/pri0000050.

13 Schalinski, I., Moran, J., Schauer, M., & Elbert, T. (2014). Raid emotional processing in relation to trauma-related symptoms as revealed by magnetic source imaging. *BMC Psychiatry, 14:193*, (1-13). http://www.biomedcentral.com/1471-244X/14/193

CHAPTER TWO

1 Damasio, A. (2012). *Self Comes to Mind: Constructing the Conscious Brain*. New York, NY: Random House.

2 Augustyn, B., Hall, T., Wang, D., & Hill, P. (2017). Relational spirituality: An attachment-based model of spiritual development and psychological well-being. *Psychology of Religion and Spirituality*, 9(2), 197-208.

3 Barnes, C. & Moodley, R. (2020). Religious change after a traumatic event within a Christian population. *British Journal of Guidance & Counselling*, 48(6), 780-790.

4 Granqvist, P. & Nkara, F. (2017). Nature meets nurture in religious and spiritual development. *British Journal of Developmental Psychology*, 35, 142-155.

5 Starnino, V. & Sullivan, W. (2016). Early trauma and serious mental illness: what role does spirituality play? *Mental Health, Religion & Culture*, 19(10), 1094-1117.

6 Frankl, V. (1988). *The Will to Meaning: Foundations and Applications of Logotherapy*. New York, NY. Penguin Group.

7 Starnino, V. (2016). When trauma, spirituality, and mental illness intersect: A qualitative case study. *Psychological Trauma: Theory, Research, Practice and Policy, 8*(3), 375-383.

8 Miller, L. (2015). *The Spiritual Child: The New Science on Parenting for Health and Lifelong Thriving.* St. Martin's Press.

9 Miller, L. (2021). *The Awakened Brain: The New Science of Spirituality and Our Quest for an Inspired Life.* Random House.

10 Taylor, J. B. (2021). *Whole Brain Living: The Anatomy of Choice and the Four Characters That Drive Our Life.* Hay House.

11 Fowler, J. (1987). *Faith Development and Pastoral Care: Theology and pastoral care.* Philadelphia, PA. Fortress Press.

12 Usset, T., Gray, E., Griffin, B., Currier, J., Kopacz, M., Wilhelm, J., & Harris, J. (2020). Psychospiritual developmental risk factors for moral injury. *Religions, 11*(10), 484-495.

CHAPTER THREE

1 Henley, T. (2019). *Hergenhahn's An Introduction to the History of Psychology,* Eight Edition. Cengage Learning, Inc. Boston, MA.

2 Ward, D. (2011). The lived experience of spiritual abuse. *Mental Health, Religion & Culture, 14*(9), 899-915.

3 Oakley, L., & Kinmond, K. (2014). Developing safeguarding policy and practice for spiritual abuse. *Journal of Adult Protection, 16*(2), 87-95.

4 Nica, A. (2019). Exiters of religious fundamentalism: reconstruction of social support and relationships related to well-being. *Mental Health, Religion, & Culture, 22*(5), 543-556.

5 History.com (2020). History of Witches. *A&E Television Networks.* Retrieved from https://www.history.com/topics/folklore/history-of-witches)

6 Lee, K. & Gubi, P. (2019). Breaking up with Jesus: A phenomenological exploration of the experience of deconversion from an Evangelical Christian faith to Atheism. *Mental Health, Religion, & Culture, 22*(2), 171-184.

7 Vanderpool, K. (2021). The age of deconstruction and future of the Church. *Relevant Magazine,* Retrieved from https://relevantmagazine.com/faith/the-age-of-deconstruction-and-future-of-the-church/

8 Mudge, M. (2021). What is faith deconstruction? *The Sophia Society*. Retrieved from https://www.sophiasociety.org/blog/what-is-faith-deconstruction

9 Winell, M. (2011). Religious trauma syndrome: It's time to recognize it. *Cognitive Behavioural Therapy Today*, 39(2), 16-18.

10 Hailes, S. (2019). Deconstructing faith: Meet the evangelicals who are questioning everything. *Premier Christianity*, Retrieved from https://www.premierchristianity.com/features/decontructing-faith-meet-the-evangelicals-who-are-questioning-everything/267.article

11 Manning, P. (2020). What the church could learn from two YouTubers losing their faith. *America, the Jesuit Review*. Retrieved from https://www.americamagazine.org/faith/2020/11/17/deconstructing-christian-faith-rhett-link-youtube-catholic

12 Onishi, B., (2019). The Rise of #Exvangelical. *Religion and Politics*. Retrieved from https://religionandpolitics.org/2019/04/09/the-rise-of-exvangelical/

13 Bielo, J. (2017). The question of cultural change in the social scientific study of religion: Notes from the emerging church. *Journal for the Scientific Study of Religion*, 56(1), 19-25.

14 Burge, R. & Djupe, P. (2017). An emergent threat: Christian clergy perceptions of the emerging church movement. *Journal for the Scientific Study of Religion*, 56(1), 26-32.

15 Marti, G. (2017). New concepts for new dynamics: Generating theory for the study of religious innovation and social change. *Journal for the Scientific Study of Religion*, 56(1), 6-18.

16 Harrold, Philip. (2006). Deconversion in the Emerging Church. *International Journal for the Study of the Christian Church* 6(1):79–90.

17 Moody, K. & Reed, R. (2017). Emerging Christianity and religious identity. *Journal for the Scientific Study of Religion*, 56(1), 33-40.

18 Conniry, C. (2008). Evangelical Christianity in America. *Faculty Publications—George Fox Evangelical Seminary*, 32, 153-160.

19 Akenson, D.H. (2020). Exporting the rapture: John Nelson Darby and the Victorian conquest of North American Evangelicalism. *American Historical Review*, 125(1), 227.

20 Akenson (2018). *Exploring the Rapture: John Nelson Darby and the Victorian Conquest of North American Evangelicalism.* New York, NY. Oxford University Press.

21 Boyer, P. (1994). *When Time Shall Be No More: Prophecy Belief in Modern American Culture.* Cambridge, MA: Harvard University Press.

22 Ryrie, C. C. (2004). *Dispensationalism: Revised and Expanded Edition.* Chicago: Moody Publishers.

23 Ellens, J. (2017). Review of When the roll is called: Trauma and the soul of American Evangelicalism. *Pastoral Psychology, 66*(4), 563-566.

24 Hoffman, M. (2016). *When the Roll is Called: Trauma and the Soul of American Evangelicalism.* Series: Fuller School of Psychology Integration Series. Cascade Books, Eugene, OR.

25 Walvoord, J. F. (1970). The dispensationalism of John Nelson Darby. *Bibliotheca Sacra, 127*(505), 35-47.

26 Darby, J. N. (2009). *The Collected Writings of J. N. Darby.* Vol. 6. [Original works compiled posthumously]. Addison, TX: Bible Truth Publishers.

27 Harrington, W. D. (2015). American apocalypse: A history of modern evangelicalism. *American Historical Review, 120*(5), 1932.

28 Hummel (2023). *The Rise and Fall of Dispensationalism. How the Evangelical Battle Over the End Times Shaped a Nation.* Grand Rapids, MI. Eerdmans Publishing Co.

29 Smidt, C. (2019). Reassessing the concept and measurement of Evangelicals: The case for the RELTRAD approach. *Journal for the Scientific Study of Religion, 58*(4), 833-853.

30 Pew Research Center. (2017, October 17). *In U.S., decline of Christianity continues at rapid pace* https://www.pewresearch.org/religion/2019/10/17/in-u-s-decline-of-christianity-continues-at-rapid-pace/

31 Steensland, B. (2019). Evangelicals, then and now: Plausibility, boundaries, and American Evangelicalism as ethnicity. *Journal for the Scientific Study of Religion, 58*(4), 921-924.

CHAPTER FOUR

1 Henley, T. (2019). *Hergenhahn's An Introduction to the History of Psychology,* Eight Edition. Cengage Learning, Inc. Boston, MA.

2 Ceylan, M., Donmez, A., Unsalver, B., Evrensel, A., & Yertutanol, F.D. (2017). The soul, as an uninhibited mental activity, is reduced into consciousness by rules of quantum physics. *Integrative Psychological & Behavioral Science, 51*, 582-597.

3 Azari, N. & Birnbacher, D. (2004). The role of cognition and feeling in religious experience. *Journal of Religion & Science, 39*(4), 901-917.

4 Miller, L. (2021). *The Awakened Brain: The New Science of Spirituality and Our Quest for an Inspired Life*. Random House.

5 Panchuk, M. (2018). The shattered spiritual self: A philosophical exploration of religious trauma. *Res Philosophica, 95*(3), 505-530.

6 Stone, A. (2013). Thou shall not: Treating religious trauma and spiritual harm with combined therapy. *International Journal of Group Psychotherapy, 37*(4), 323-337.

7 Winell, M. (2011). Religious trauma syndrome: It's time to recognize it. *Cognitive Behavioural Therapy Today, 39*(2), 16-18.

8 Ward, D. (2011). The lived experience of spiritual abuse. *Mental Health, Religion & Culture, 14*(9), 899-915.

9 Gubi, P. & Jacobs, R. (2009). Exploring the impact on counsellors of working with spiritually abused clients. *Mental Health, Religion & Culture, 12*(2), 191-204.

10 Oakley, L.R., Kinmond, K., & Humphreys, J. (2018). Spiritual abuse in the Christian faith settings: Definition, policy and practice guidance. *Journal of Adult Protection, 20*(3/4), 144-154.

11 Simonic, B., Mandelj, T., & Novsak, R. (2013). Religious-related abuse in the family. *Journal of Family Violence, 28*, 339-349.

12 Lee, K. & Gubi, P. (2019). Breaking up with Jesus: A phenomenological exploration of the experience of deconversion from an Evangelical Christian faith to Atheism. *Mental Health, Religion, & Culture, 22*(2), 171-184.

13 Hoffman, M. (2016). *When the Roll is Called: Trauma and the Soul of American Evangelicalism*. Series: Fuller School of Psychology Integration Series. Cascade Books, Eugene, OR.

14 Koch, D, & Edstrom, L. (2022). Development of the spiritual harm and abuse scale. *Journal for the Scientific Study of Religion, 61*(2), 476-506.

15 Ayrapetova, A. (2020). Indoctrination as a mechanism of psychological manipulation in the process of involvement in destructive religious organizations. *European Journal of Research and Reflection in Educational Sciences, 8*(11), 17-23.

16 Milstead, K. (2021). Why cognitive dissonance is so traumatic for survivors of pathological love relationships. Retrieved December 9, 2022 from https://survivortreatment.com/why-cognitive-dissonance-is-so-traumatic/

17 Aronson, E. & Carlsmith, J.M. (1963). Effect of the severity of threat on the devaluation of forbidden behavior. *Journal of Abnormal and Social Psychology, 66*, 584-588.

18 Cashwell, C., Myers, J., & Shurts, W.M. (2004). Using the developmental counseling and therapy model to work with a client in spiritual bypass: Some preliminary considerations. *Journal of Counseling & Development, 82*, 403-409.

19 Fox, J. & Picciotto, G. (2019). The mediating effects of spiritual bypass on depression, anxiety, and stress. *Counseling & Values, 64*, 227-245.

20 Picciotto, G. & Fox, J. (2018). Exploring experts' perspectives on spiritual bypass: a conventional content analysis. *Pastoral Psychology, 67*, 65-84.

21 Llyod, C.E.M. & Waller, R. (2020). Demon? Disorder? Or none of the above? A survey for the attitudes and experiences of evangelical Christians with mental distress. *Mental Health, Religion & Culture, 23*(8), 679-690.

22 Dominguez, K. (2018). Encountering disenfranchised grief: An investigation of the clinical lived experiences in dance/movement therapy. *American Journal of Dance Therapy, 40*, 254-276.

CHAPTER FIVE

1 Spilka, B., Shaver, P. & Kirkpatrick, L. (1985). A general attribution theory for the psychology of religion. *Journal for the Scientific Study of Religion, 24*(1), 1-20.

2 Weiner, B. (2018). The legacy of an attribution approach to motivation and emotion: A no-crisis zone. *Motivation Science, 4*(1), 4-14.

3 Dweck, C. (2018). Reflections of the legacy of attribution theory. *Motivational Science, 4*(1), 17-18.

4 Eccles, J. & Wigfield, A. (2002). Motivational beliefs, values, and goals. *Annual Review of Psychology, 53*, 109-32.

5 Hareli, S. & Hess, U. (2008). The role of causal attributions in hurt feelings and related social emotions elicited in reaction to other's feedback about failure. *Cognition and Emotion, 22*(5), 862-880.

6 Shortz, J. & Worthington, Jr, E. (1994). Young adults' recall religiosity, attributions, and coping in parental divorce. *Journal for the Scientific Study of Religion, 33*(2), 172-179.

7 Granqvist, P. (2007). Invited Essay: On the relation between secular and Divine relationships: An emerging attachment perspective and a critique of the 'depth' approaches. *The International Journal for the Psychology of Religion, 16*(1), 1-18.

8 Pargament K. I. (2007) *Spiritually Integrated Psychotherapy: Understanding and Addressing the Sacred*, New York, Guilford.

9 Siegel, D. (2001). Toward an interpersonal neurobiology of the developing mind: Attachment relationships, "mindsight," and neural integration. *Infant Mental Health Journal, 22(1-2)*, 67-94.

10 Barnes, C. & Moodley, R. (2020). Religious change after a traumatic event within a Christian population. *British Journal of Guidance & Counselling, 48*(6), 780-790.

11 Starnino, V. & Sullivan, W. (2016). Early trauma and serious mental illness: what role does spirituality play? *Mental Health, Religion & Culture, 19*(10), 1094-1117.

12 Fowler, J. (1996). *Faithful Change: The Personal and Public Challenges of Postmodern Life.* Nashville, TN. Abingdon Press.

13 Freeman, N. & Baldwin, I. (2020). Attitudes toward mental illness in American Evangelical communities, supernaturalism, and stigmatization. *Mental Health, Religion & Culture, 23*(8), 691-702.

14 Kam, C. (2018). Integrating Divine attachment theory and the Enneagram to help clients of abuse heal in their images of self, others, and God. *Pastoral Psychology, 67,* 341-356.

15 Leman, J., Hunter III, W., Fergus, T., & Rowatt, W. (2018). Secure attachment to God uniquely linked to psychological health in a national random sample of American adults. *The International Journal for the Psychology of Religion, 28*(3), 162-173.

16 Cherniak, A., Mikulincer, M., Shaver, P., & Granqvist, P. (2021). Attachment theory and religion. *Current Opinion in Psychology, 40*, 126-130.

17 Desai, K. & Pargament, K. (2015). Predictors of growth and decline following spiritual struggles. *The International Journal for the Psychology of Religion, 25*, 42-56.

18 Fowler, J. (1981). *Stages of Faith: The Psychology of human development and the quest for meaning.* New York, NY. HarperCollins.

19 Stone, A. (2013). Thou shall not: Treating religious trauma and spiritual harm with combined therapy. *International Journal of Group Psychotherapy, 37*(4), 323-337.

CHAPTER SIX

1 Fowler, J. (1996). *Faithful Change: The Personal and Public Challenges of Postmodern Life.* Nashville, TN. Abingdon Press.

2 Henley, T. (2019). *Hergenhahn's An Introduction to the History of Psychology,* Eight Edition. Cengage Learning, Inc. Boston, MA.

CHAPTER SEVEN

1 Ehrman, B. D. (2003). *Lost Christianities: The Battles for Scripture and the Faiths We Never Knew.* Oxford University Press.

2 Gonzalez, J. L. (1984). *Story of Christianity: Volume 1, The: The Early Church to the Dawn of the Reformation.* HarperOne.

3 Ehrman, B. D. (2020). *Heaven and Hell: A History of the Afterlife.* Simon & Schuster.

4 Pagels, E. (1979). *The Gnostic Gospels.* Random House.

5 Pagels, E. (1988). *Adam, Eve, and the Serpent: Sex and Politics in Early Christianity.* Vintage.

CHAPTER EIGHT

1 Ehrman, B. D. (2003). *Lost Christianities: The Battles for Scripture and the Faiths We Never Knew.* Oxford University Press.

2 Gonzalez, J. L. (1984). *Story of Christianity: Volume 1, The: The Early Church to the Dawn of the Reformation.* HarperOne.

3 Ehrman, B. D. (2020). *Heaven and Hell: A History of the Afterlife*. Simon & Schuster.

4 Pagels, E. (1979). *The Gnostic Gospels*. Random House.

5 Pagels, E. (1988). *Adam, Eve, and the Serpent: Sex and Politics in Early Christianity*. Vintage.

6 Pagels, E. H. (2003). *Beyond Belief: The Secret Gospel of Thomas*. Random House.

7 Heiser, M. S. (2015). *The Unseen Realm: Recovering the Supernatural Worldview of the Bible*. Lexham Press.

8 Bar, E. (2023). *The "Gospel" of Divine Abuse: Redeeming the Gospel from Gruesome Popular Preaching of an Abusive and Violent God*. Shamus; 2nd edition.

9 Hart, D. B. (2019). *That All Shall Be Saved: Heaven, Hell, and Universal Salvation*. Yale University Press.

10 Bar, E. (2024). *HELL: A Jewish Perspective on a Christian Doctrine*. Shamus Magnificient Books.

Expanded Perspectives
Recommended Reading & Listening

This is a beginning to your journey. You have permission to question and you have the freedom to forge your own path to healing. The following books and podcasts are a starting point to help you find what resonates within you—a place to find your inner wisdom.

*Listen to what awakens your Soul—
follow your own path and **trust yourself**.*

RECOMMENDED READING

Dr. Eitan Bar
- *Hell: A Jewish Perspective on a Christian Doctrine*

Dr. Elaine Pagels
- *The Gnostic Gospels*
- *Beyond Belief: The Secret Gospel of Thomas*
- *The Origin of Satan: How Christians Demonized Jews, Pagans, and Heretics*
- *Revelations: Visions, Prophesy, and Politics in the Book of Revelation*

Dr. Bart Ehrman
- *Misquoting Jesus: The Story Behind Who Changed the Bible and Why*
- *Lost Christianities: The Battle for Scripture and the Faiths We Never Knew*
- *Jesus, Interrupted: Revealing the Hidden Contradictions in the Bible*

Dr. Michael S. Heiser
- *The Unseen Realm: Recovering the Supernatural World View of the Bible*
- *Reversing Herman: Enoch, the Watchers, and the Forgotten Message of Jesus Christ*
- *Supernatural: What the Bible Teaches About the Unseen World and Why it Matters*

Dr. David Bentley Hart
- *That All Shall Be Saved: Heaven, Hell, and Universal Salvation*

Dr. Lisa Miller
- *The Awakened Brain*
- *The Spiritual Child*

Dr. Jill Bolte Taylor
- *Whole Brain Living*

Dr. Eben Alexander
- *Proof of Heaven: A Neurosurgeon's Journey into the Afterlife*

Dr. Marie Hoffman
- *When the Roll is Called: Trauma and the Soul of American Evangelicalism*

Marshall Davis
- *The Gospel of Nonduality: A Spiritual Interpretation of the Gospel of John*

William G. Duffy
- *The Hidden Gospel of Thomas: Commentaries of the Non-Dual Sayings of Jesus*

Jim Palmer, *Former Megachurch Pastor*
- *Being Jesus in Nashville*
- *Notes From (Over) the Edge*
- *Inner Anarchy*

Keith Giles, *Former Pastor*
- *The Unseries (several books)*

Michael Singer
- *The Untethered Soul*
- *Living Untethered*

RECOMMENDED LISTENING & PODCASTS

Deconstruction & Healing from Spiritual Abuse

- *The New Evangelicals Podcast* – Hosted by Tim Whitaker, this podcast explores deconstruction, faith shifts, and church trauma with honesty and compassion.
- *The Messy Spirituality Podcast* – Focuses on grace, authenticity, and healing for those who feel disillusioned by organized religion.
- *Exvangelical* – Hosted by Blake Chastain, this podcast features interviews with those who have left Evangelicalism and are reclaiming their faith or spirituality.
- *Faith Unleashed with Keith Giles* – Addresses leaving fundamentalism and rediscovering Jesus outside of toxic church systems.
- *Dirty Rotten Church Kids* – Two former church kids share their humorous yet insightful take on leaving Evangelicalism and embracing freedom.
- *Bodies Behind the Bus* – Provides a platform for individuals to reclaim their narratives and shed light on the epidemic of abuse within Western evangelical spaces.
- *The Liturgists Podcast* – Covers spirituality, faith shifts, and deconstruction with intellectual and emotional depth.
- *Almost Heretical* – A deep dive into biblical interpretations and theology that challenge harmful church teachings.
- *Heretic Happy Hour* – Engages in open and irreverent discussions on deconstruction, theology, and grace.
- *Reclaiming My Theology* – Explores how theology has been used to harm and how to reclaim a faith that aligns with love and justice.
- *The Deconstructionists Podcast* – Explores faith deconstruction while still embracing Jesus in a more mystical, love-centered way.

Mystical Christianity & Christ Consciousness

Cynthia Bourgeault – The Wisdom Way of Knowing
- A modern Christian mystic and contemplative teacher, Cynthia explores Centering Prayer, non-dual Christianity, and *The Gospel of Thomas*.
- Podcast: Guest appearances on *Turning to the Mystics* and *The Liturgists*.
- Books: *The Wisdom Jesus, Centering Prayer and Inner Awakening*

Richard Rohr – Another Name for Every Thing
- Franciscan priest and founder of the Center for Action and Contemplation, Rohr speaks on non-dual Christianity, mysticism, and Divine Love.
- Podcast: *Another Name for Every Thing* (with the Center for Action & Contemplation).
- Book: *The Universal Christ*

YOUTUBE CHANNELS

These channels can be incredibly empowering for those who are healing from spiritual abuse, moving beyond restrictive belief systems, and embracing a higher consciousness rooted in love and freedom.

Aaron Abke

Raised in a devout Christian home as the son of a pastor, Aaron was deeply immersed in Evangelical theology from a young age. He later became a worship pastor himself, passionately seeking to deepen his relationship with God. However, after experiencing a profound spiritual awakening, he began to question the fear-based doctrines he had been taught.

Aaron Abke focuses on spiritual awakening, consciousness, and non-dual teachings through a blend of Christian mysticism, metaphysics, and the Law of One. His content resonates with those who are deconstructing religious belief systems while still seeking a deep and authentic connection with God, Christ, and the higher self. His YouTube channel and podcast are great resources for shifting from fear-based religion to love-centered spirituality.

The JESUS Way Podcast

Danny Morel

Danny Morel is a transformational coach and speaker who focuses on spiritual growth, self-healing, and abundance. He often discusses breaking free from limiting beliefs, including those rooted in religious trauma, and stepping into personal empowerment and Divine Love. His approach blends mindset, spirituality, and practical tools for inner transformation.

The Higher Self Podcast

Acknowledgments

This process of writing *The Forgotten Self*—birthed from the qualitative research of my doctorate—has been an endeavor made possible only by those who have stood beside me over these past few years.

My deepest appreciation goes to my mentor and Chair, Dr. Tara Zolnikov, whose unwavering belief in this message has carried me forward. Your encouragement, insight, and uncompromising support have been foundational to bringing this work to life.

To Lexi, my editor and interior design visionary—thank you for the countless hours spent revising, refining, and creating. You shaped draft after draft with such care and devotion until this book became what it is now, ready to be held in the hands of those who need it. This book would not exist without your brilliance.

To my clients throughout the years, and to the participants in my research—thank you for your courage. You have faced your pain, your trauma, and your stories with honesty and openness. You allowed me access into the most sacred places of your thoughts, emotions, and hearts. I am profoundly grateful for your trust, and for your belief that healing is possible.

To my sister, my brother, my mother, and my husband—thank you for sitting with me for hours, helping me shape this message so it could move from academic language into something that could truly be heard. Thank you for reading every word, for your encouragement, and for believing in both me and the purpose of this project.

Your support has been a steady presence, and I could not have completed this work without each of you.

And to the two Beautiful Souls that forever changed my life—my children Jared Franklin and Jordin Jene. You are who taught me what Love feels like. Thank you for believing in me from the very beginning. Thank you for your constant encouragement and your unconditional love and support. You are my greatest Joy and Inspiration. I love you Bunches and Bunches - With All My Heart - Always and Always - No Matter What.

My success is shared with you—for we did this together.

About the Author

DR. CRISTY S. CARR is a clinical psychologist and trauma specialist with nearly two decades of experience supporting individuals through deep psychological and spiritual healing. A certified Brainspotting Practitioner, she has been integrating this powerful, somatic-based modality into her work for over seven years to help clients access and resolve trauma stored in the body and nervous system. She is deeply invested in understanding how rigid religious systems can harm individuals psychologically, emotionally, and spiritually, and her work focuses on the healing process for those who have been harmed by these systems.

Carr's approach combines clinical psychology with a compassionate, trauma-informed perspective. She works to help individuals untangle the complex emotions tied to their past religious experiences, addressing issues such as shame, guilt, identity loss, and cognitive dissonance. Her work is also centered on empowering individuals to rediscover their own sense of self-worth and spiritual identity after experiencing the trauma of spiritual abuse. Her therapeutic work often involves helping clients reclaim their autonomy and develop a more authentic, individualized spiritual journey.

Dr. Carr emphasizes the importance of moving beyond the constraints of rigid religious structures to find healing and peace, guiding clients to trust their own intuition and internal compass. She is dedicated to fostering environments where clients can process their experiences, question old beliefs without fear of judgment, and ultimately rebuild a spirituality that aligns with their true selves.

Dr. Carr's voice is compassionate and empathetic, yet grounded in clinical expertise. She encourages people to be patient with themselves and to view the journey of healing as an ongoing, non-linear process. Her work serves as both a form of therapeutic guidance and a resource for those navigating the painful, but transformative, experience of leaving spiritually abusive environments.

Additional Books & Resources from Dr. Cristy S. Carr

A Journey Back to Love: Return to the Love That Never Left

A gentle, soul-guided path for those healing from the wounds of religious fear, spiritual abuse, or the ache of feeling exiled from God. This book is a living invitation to remember the Love that has always been calling you home.

The Uncharted Self: From Certainty to Soul

A soul-centered companion for those moving beyond religious trauma, offering a gentle path through questioning, grief, and spiritual awakening.

For more information or purchase options, please visit:
AutotelicLife.com

www.ingramcontent.com/pod-product-compliance
Lightning Source LLC
Chambersburg PA
CBHW020538030426
42337CB00013B/892